Weaning
Made
Easy
Recipes

Weaning Made Easy Recipes

150 simple and tasty ideas for spoon-feeding and baby-led weaning

Dr Rana Conway PhD RNutr (Public Health)

white
LADDER

Important note

The information in this book is not intended as a substitute for medical advice. Neither the author nor White Ladder can accept any responsibility for any injury, damages or losses suffered as a result of following the information herein.

Weaning Made Easy Recipes: 150 simple and tasty ideas for spoon-feeding and baby-led weaning

This first edition published in 2014 by White Ladder Press, an imprint of Crimson Publishing Ltd, The Tramshed, Walcot Street, Bath BA1 5BB.

British Library Cataloguing in Publication Data
A catalogue record for this book is available from the British Library.

ISBN 978 1 908281 74 6

Typeset by IDS UK (DataConnections) Ltd
Printed and bound in Malta by Gutenberg Press Ltd, Malta

Contents

About the author   vii

Acknowledgements   ix

1. **Weaning when, what and how?**   1
    What is weaning?   2
    When should you start weaning?   2
    How to feed your baby   3
    Drinks   11
    Supplements   12
    Foods to avoid   13
    Preparing food for your baby   15
    Feeding your baby   16
    Allergies and food intolerances   17
    Kitchen equipment   18
    Buying food   19
    Planning meals   20
    Happy cooking!   21
    Author's recipe notes   21
    Conversion chart   23

2. **Feeding your 4- to 6-month old**   24
    Purées   25
    Fingers foods   25
    Breakfasts   26
    Lunches and dinners   29
    Puddings and snacks   50
    Meal plan for a 6-month-old baby   57
    Dos, don'ts and FAQs   59

3. **Feeding your 7- to 9-month-old**   63
    Breakfasts   64

Lunches and dinners 67

Puddings and snacks 95

Meal plan for a 7- to 9-month-old baby 103

Dos, don'ts and FAQs 106

4. Feeding your 10- to 12-month-old 110

Breakfasts 111

Lunches and dinners 114

Puddings and snacks 142

Meal plan for a 10- to 9-month-old baby 150

Dos, don'ts and FAQs 152

5. Feeding your toddler and beyond 156

Breakfasts 157

Lunches and dinners 160

Puddings and snacks 185

Fruit smoothies, shakes and lassis 193

Meal plan for a toddler 195

Dos, don'ts and FAQs 197

List of recipes with dietary restrictions 200

Index 208

About the author

Rana Conway is a Registered Nutritionist and a member of the Nutrition Society. Over the past 20 years she has established herself as an expert in nutrition for pregnancy and childhood. She has carried out nutrition research at leading universities and her work with pregnant women earned her a PhD in 1997.

Rana has also lectured on a wide range of undergraduate courses and has taught nutrition to medical students, midwives and trainee dieticians. As well as writing books and research papers, Rana is the nutrition expert for *Practical Parenting & Pregnancy* magazine and writes for the NCT. Her first book on weaning, *Weaning Made Easy*, was published by White Ladder in October 2011.

She lives in London with her husband and their three children.

Acknowledgements

Many thanks to Beth Bishop at White Ladder for her enthusiasm for the book, sharing her own weaning experiences with me and helping with recipe testing. Also to Jane Graham Maw and Jennifer Christie at Graham Maw Christie for their help and Adam Hargrave at the Food Standards Agency for answering the food safety questions that nobody else can answer. Thank you too to Susi Elmer (Crimson Publishing), Rosie Wright (Rosie Wright's Weaning Workshops), Suzie Walker (Wonders of Food), Adele Stevenson (Baby Led Workshops) and my husband Olly for his support and encouragement, even when given baby beef stew for dinner.

A very big thank you to those who tested recipes and gave invaluable feedback: Sophie Barker, Emma Bertuzzi, Christine Callod, Daniel Conway, Joseph Conway, Madeleine Conway, Nick Conway, Vanessa Conway, Carolyn Dajani, Lauren Daly, Mary Drake, Nikki Duffy, Gilda Gutierrez, Claire Hall, Sarah Harris, Vanessa Heaney, Tom Howse, Emma James, Lorelei Jones, Charlotte Kenyon, Claudine Love, Katherine Lyons, Jessica McCallin, Emma McEwan, Ellie McGrath, Laura Miranda, Zuzanna Nowak, Nancy Shaw, Monika Tomaszewska, Cally Trewren and Charlie Walton. And of course to the babies and toddlers who were the real testers and who gave their very honest opinions.

1 Weaning: when, what and how?

Babies start eating solid foods in a variety of ways and at a range of different ages. Some begin with purées at 4 months and others with a slice of toast at 8 months. There is no single right way to feed your baby, but there are guidelines that can help you ensure successful weaning.

During weaning you are aiming to make sure your baby:

- gets all the nutrients needed for health, growth and development
- does not have too much salt or sugar, which can lead to health problems
- avoids anything that could cause food poisoning
- does not develop a taste for unhealthy processed foods
- learns to enjoy healthy natural food.

Achieving these aims isn't as complicated as you might think, but it does require a bit of effort and forward planning. Below you'll find a brief explanation of when to start weaning and the different options, including traditional and baby-led weaning. A fuller explanation is found in my first book in this series, *Weaning Made Easy* (White Ladder, 2011), along with more detailed advice about allergies and feeding problems. In this book you will find plenty of recipes to suit your baby, whichever method you've chosen and whatever particular needs she may have.

Some babies take to solids easily and are soon gobbling up chicken stew and whole apples. Others make a meal of a tiny rice cake. You can't fight your baby's nature and there's no need to try. It's all about finding what works for you. Relax, embrace the fact that your baby is an individual and enjoy the journey together.

What is weaning?

In the UK (and in this book) 'weaning' means the introduction of solids or real foods to your baby's diet. In the United States and some other countries the term 'weaning' refers to stopping breastfeeding or formula feeding. Often, these two developments happen at the same time: as babies eat increasing amounts of solids over a period of about 18 months, they need less milk. But the two do not need to go hand in hand and should be considered separately. If you are breastfeeding your baby, that is great – ideally you should continue to do this while you introduce a range of different foods. Likewise, if you give your baby formula milk, she should continue to have this as her main drink until she is a year old.

When should you start weaning?

The Department of Health recommends the introduction of solid foods 'at around 6 months of age'. This is interpreted by some parents and health workers as meaning that 6 months is the absolute minimum age. However, this is not the case. The official guidelines, which came out in 2003, state that 'all infants are individuals and will require a flexible approach'. If a baby is showing signs of being ready to start solids before 6 months, this should be encouraged, says the advice.

> ## Signs that your baby is ready for solids
> - Sitting up with support
> - Holding her head up without support
> - Not seeming satisfied after a milk feed
> - Showing an interest in other people eating
> - Trying to pick up and taste food
> - Making chewing motions
>
> Waking in the night is sometimes taken as another sign, but this is very common in babies between 3 and 5 months, and weaning is unlikely to help.

There is quite a lot of debate among health professionals and other experts about whether it is really necessary to wait until 6 months to start weaning, but there is agreement that 4 months is the absolute earliest age. Babies should not be given any food other than breast milk or formula before

4 months (17 weeks). Babies who are weaned earlier than this are more likely to become overweight and are at increased risk of getting infections and developing allergies.

Starting the weaning process much later than 6 months can also cause problems and isn't advisable. When babies are about 6 months old they start to need more than milk alone can provide. If they don't begin to have other foods they can be at increased risk of micronutrient deficiencies such as iron deficiency.

How to feed your baby

There are two basic approaches to weaning: the traditional way, where you start by offering purées, and the baby-led method. Both have pros and cons, and there are plenty of parents who'll tell you that their system is wonderful and the other leads to disaster. In truth, different approaches suit different parents and different babies. An increasing number of parents appear to be taking a bit from each method and doing what works best for them.

Traditional weaning involves feeding a baby puréed food with a spoon. In the past few decades, when most babies were weaned at around 4 months, this was the way it was usually done, and it is still the most common approach. Generally, you start with baby rice mixed with milk, followed by smooth puréed carrot, apple or pear. Once babies are used to smooth purées, at 6–7 months, they move on to lumpier purées and are introduced to a wider range of foods, including meat, fish, eggs and cheese. Babies then gradually move on to mashed, followed by chopped, meals and have an increasingly wide variety of flavours and textures, including a range of finger foods, until they are eating the same dishes as the rest of the family.

Baby-led weaning (BLW) doesn't involve any spoon-feeding by a parent. Instead, babies are given pieces of food to hold and they feed themselves. This means babies don't have puréed food, but instead can join in family meals. Giving babies 'choice' and 'control' is central to the idea of BLW. The theory is that by doing this babies won't become fussy eaters. It is certainly true that babies shouldn't be forced to eat anything, but this can also be avoided in traditional weaning by spoon-feeding in a responsive way. There are many other claims about BLW helping with speech and co-ordination, but these are not backed by evidence.

If you want to try BLW, don't be put off by those who insist it can only be done in a certain way (for example, never with a spoon as this is equated with force-feeding). This method has lots to offer and even if you decide to start with purées there are useful tips to be taken from BLW. Also, your baby may disagree with your choice to spoon-feed and decide herself that BLW is better.

Traditional weaning with purées

Main features

- Start by giving your baby purées, then move on in stages to lumpier food.
- Feed your baby with a spoon.
- Start with simple foods, such as apple and carrot, then gradually move on to mixed meals and different flavours.
- Give finger foods as snacks or only as part of a meal (e.g. pudding).

Advantages

- You can feed a baby whether or not she has the skills to feed herself.
- It's easier to plan a balanced diet and disguise certain foods if you want to.
- You can use jars or pouches, which can be more convenient sometimes.
- It's easier to see what's been eaten.

Disadvantages

- Preparing special meals is time-consuming, and it can be stressful if they're not eaten.
- Some babies have problems moving from smooth purées to lumps.
- Babies can be overfed.
- Moving from special baby meals or jars to family meals can be difficult.

Baby-led weaning

Main features

- No spoon-feeding with purées.
- Babies feed themselves with their hands.

- Babies choose what to eat at family meals.
- They choose how much to eat without any coaxing.

Advantages

- The baby has more control at mealtimes and overfeeding is unlikely.
- There are no purées or special meals to make.
- Problems moving from purées to lumps are avoided.
- It encourages babies to share family meals and therefore develop healthier eating habits and avoid fussiness.

Disadvantages

- Adult foods can be too salty, spicy or tough.
- Babies miss out on foods they can't feed themselves (e.g. yogurt or porridge) and therefore miss certain nutrients.
- It's messy and meals can take a long time.
- It doesn't suit all babies as it's difficult for many at 6 months and for those with developmental delays.

As you can see, there are pros and cons to both, which may make it difficult to decide what to do for the best. Many parents choose the bits from each method that make sense to them and take a more balanced approach. This might involve feeding their baby some mashed-up shepherd's pie while also giving her broccoli florets to feed herself. Or sharing pieces of omelette and fruit together at lunchtime, but feeding her mashed chicken casserole in the evening when she's feeling tired.

When it comes to choosing between purées or BLW there is no proof that either is better. However, there is evidence that the way you go about weaning can affect your baby's nutrient intake and relationship with food in the long term. To get the best out of weaning, you should follow the tips listed below.

- Let your baby decide when she's had enough. Don't coax or play games; babies can be overfed or fight back and become fussier.
- Eat together and have the same food whenever possible. This has been found to increase long-term healthy eating.
- Make every bite count. Babies should have some choice, but only from a range of healthy foods. They shouldn't fill up on milk or snacks between meals.

- Encourage your baby to experiment and try different foods even if she just plays with them.
- Expect your baby to eat much less some days than others, to suddenly go off her favourite food, or to decide that she won't let you spoon-feed her. Try to relax, be flexible and think long term.

Foods for babies

	Why they're good	How to eat them
Fruit and vegetables	**They're packed with vitamins, phytochemicals and fibre.**	**Fresh, puréed, dried, tinned, stewed, baked in cakes and puddings, in jars, pots or pouches.**
Apples	Help protect against asthma and allergies.	Stewed (p51) or in mixed desserts (p95) or older babies can have them raw.
Bananas	Good for potassium, vitamin B6 and a prebiotic for digestive health.	Mashed or whole for breakfast, pudding or snacks, or cooked in cakes (p102) and desserts (p99).
Berries and currants (e.g. raspberries)	Rich in antioxidant nutrients, especially vitamin C, and a range of cancer-fighting phytochemicals.	Large strawberries can be given whole, but smaller fruits should be sliced or mashed. Also good in purées, cakes and puddings (p142).
Citrus fruit (e.g. oranges)	Rich in vitamin C and other organic acids that boost iron absorption.	Older babies can suck on washed and quartered oranges, or put them in a fruit salad.
Pears	Help with constipation.	Raw, puréed (p29) or in puddings (p187).
Rhubarb	Rich in cancer-fighting polyphenols.	Stewed, in a crumble (p95) or with yogurt.

Stone fruits (e.g. apricots, mango, peaches)	Orange varieties are rich in beta-carotene, for immunity and eye health.	Whole (with stone removed), puréed, in fruit salads, stewed and in puddings (p55).
Tropical fruit (e.g. pineapple, kiwi)	Rich in vitamin C and fibre.	Raw, in fruit salads or in cakes or puddings (p99).
Asparagus	Rich in folate, for new cell production, including blood cells, and for growth.	Steamed or baked (p37).
Aubergine	May help stabilise blood glucose levels.	Stewed (p76).
Avocado	Rich in potassium and monounsaturated fat, so they add calories to purées as well as creaminess.	As finger food – sliced (with or without skin), mashed or as a purée (p31) or dip (p43).
Beetroot	Rich in potassium to counteract the effects of salt, and also in antioxidants.	In a mixed purée or dip (p120) or grated and added to chocolate cake.
Broccoli, cauliflower, spinach and greens	Good for vitamin C and iron (although the iron in spinach is hard to absorb).	Steamed, boiled, stir-fried, puréed (p29), with pasta (p87) or in mixed dishes (p47).
Carrots, pumpkin and squashes	Provide beta-carotene, and are also sweet so are popular with babies.	Steamed, boiled, roasted (p35), in stews (p49), soups (p72) and cakes (p149).
Celery and fennel	Provide fibre and a new flavour.	In soup, pasta sauce (p171) or braised with cheese.
Courgettes	Provide folate and vitamin C.	Puréed (p33), in fritters (p73) or grated into cake mixture.
Cucumber	High water content and easy to prepare.	In sticks, peeled for younger babies.

Continued over page

Weaning Made Easy Recipes

Continued from overleaf

	Why they're good	How to eat them
Onions, leeks, chives and garlic	Known as allium vegetables, they protect against stomach and colon cancer and help to flavour mixed dishes.	In purées, pasta sauces (p38), stir-fries, soups and stews.
Peas and beans	Good source of protein without the saturated fat found in meat and dairy foods. Peas also provide vitamin C.	In purées (p43), pasta sauces (p130) and mixed dishes.
Peppers (e.g. red pepper)	Rich in vitamin C and other antioxidants.	Puréed (p30), stir-fried (p179), with rice (p128), fish (p83) and in pasta sauce (p38).
Root vegetables (e.g. celeriac, swede, parsnip)	Nutritious, fairly sweet and easy to purée.	In purées (p29), roasted (p35) or in mixed dishes.
Tomatoes	Rich in antioxidants including vitamin C and lycopene.	Raw with lunch or in a salad (p165). Tinned in soups (p122) and stews.
Protein foods	**Protein is needed for growth.**	**It's good to have a little with most meals.**
Beef, lamb and pork	Rich in iron and zinc as well as protein.	In stews (p49), patties (p88), burgers (p182) and meatballs (p137).
Chicken	Easier to digest than red meat and good for iron and zinc.	Roast, stir-fried (p179), stewed (p89, p180), with couscous (p177) or pasta (p87).

Oily fish (e.g. salmon, mackerel, sardines, trout, fresh tuna)	Rich in long-chain omega 3 fatty acids, which are important for brain and eye development. Also iron and vitamins A and D.	Grilled (p84), in fish pie (p84), patties, rösti, pasta sauce, pâté (p161) or dip. (1–2 portions per week are recommended.)
White fish (e.g. cod, coley, tinned tuna)	Rich in iodine, to help regulate metabolism, and selenium, for a healthy immune system.	In purée, fish pie (p84), pasta sauce, tuna melt (p162) or fish cakes (p132).
Tofu	Good alternative to meat and a source of calcium.	In stir-fries and patties (p127).
Eggs	Excellent source of vitamins B2, B12 and D. Good for binding together patties and pancakes.	Scrambled (p45), hard-boiled, in omelettes (p81), tortilla and pancakes.
Beans and chickpeas	Good for iron and fibre as well as protein. Convenient and cheap compared with meat, especially when tinned.	In dips (p120), pasta sauce (p130), finger foods (p75) and mixed dishes (p177). Best with foods rich in vitamin C to promote iron absorption.
Lentils	Provide iron, selenium and slow-release energy. Easier to digest than beans.	In stews (p78), pasta sauce and soups (p122).
Nuts	Provide protein, essential fatty acids and vitamins B6 and E.	Chopped or ground for under-3s. In burgers (p119), breakfasts (p158) and baking (p191).
Seeds	Packed with nutrients and essential fatty acids.	As oils, such as rapeseed oil, or ground so that the nutrients are accessible.

Continued over page

Weaning Made Easy Recipes

Continued from overleaf

	Why they're good	How to eat them
Starchy foods	Needed for energy as well as supplying fibre and some protein.	Give some with every meal. Include both wholegrain and refined products.
Bread	Provide iron and vitamin B6. Wholegrain varieties supply fibre.	As sandwiches and toast, but can be quite salty, so limit intake or make low salt versions (p70).
Breakfast cereals	Many are fortified with iron and B vitamins.	For breakfast or a snack.
Oats	Excellent for B vitamins, soluble fibre and slow-release carbohydrate.	As porridge (p65), porridge fingers (p26) or muesli, in baking (p144) and savoury dishes (p132).
Potatoes, including sweet potatoes	Supply vitamin C. Sweet potatoes provide beta-carotene as well.	Boiled, baked, mashed, roast, and in pancakes (p140) or muffins (p147).
Rice, pasta, couscous and bulgur	Provide a range of vitamins and minerals as well as carbohydrates.	In a wide variety of savoury and sweet dishes.
Milk and dairy foods	**Provide energy, protein, calcium and B vitamins.**	**Full-fat products are best until your child is 2.**
Breast milk and formula	Designed to meet all a baby's nutritional needs until she is about 6 months old.	As your baby's main drink until at least her first birthday.
Cows' milk	Provides calcium and the majority of essential nutrients.	In small amounts in foods but not as a drink until at least a year old.
Yogurt and fromage frais	Supply the same nutrients as milk, plus probiotics.	Plain, full-fat versions on their own or mixed with fruit or as dips.

Hard cheeses	Very high in calcium (but also high in salt).	In small amounts with mixed dishes or as finger food.
Cream cheese	Lower in salt but also in calcium.	On bread or toast and in sauces (p39) and spreads (p161).
Fats	**Needed for essential fatty acids and fat-soluble vitamins A, D, E and K. Also to meet babies' high energy demands.**	**Fatty meat and snack foods should be avoided but babies need healthier fats, such as those found in oily fish and certain vegetable oils.**
Sesame and flax seed oils	Provide short-chain omega 3 fatty acids to help balance high intakes of omega 6.	Salad dressings or dips.
Rapeseed oil	Contains less saturated fat than butter or olive oil.	For frying and baking.
Olive oil	Higher in monounsaturated fats than other oils and fats.	For cooking at lower temperatures when making pasta sauces, etc.

Drinks

Until your baby is 12 months old, her main drink should be breast milk or infant formula. Cows' milk is not suitable for babies as a main drink until they are at least a year old as it contains too much sodium and not enough of the essential nutrients your baby needs, including iron. The same goes for goats' milk, sheep's milk and milk substitutes made from soya or oats. However, from 6 months, small amounts of cows' milk are ok, for example in cheese sauce.

Milk facts

- Until their first birthday, babies need 500–600ml of milk each day.
- This should be breast milk or infant formula.
- Exclusively breastfed babies need between three and five feeds a day once they reach 6 months and are having solids.
- Babies under 6 months shouldn't have formula labelled as 'follow-on' or 'good night' milk. There are no proven health benefits of giving it to older babies either.
- Babies who are 12 months old or older need just 300–350ml of milk a day.
- Giving babies more than the recommended amount of milk can put them off eating solids, which can mean they miss out on essential nutrients such as iron and vitamin C.

When babies start to have solids it's very important to offer them water and encourage them to drink it. If not, there's a risk that they'll become constipated. Some babies start by having water in a bottle, but ideally they should be having it from a cup. It takes some babies a while to get the hang of drinking water from a cup, but even if they appear to be getting virtually nothing to start with, keep persevering. Offer a cup of water with each meal and snack, and even in between. Cups with a valve to stop spills are ok for babies once they're older, but it can be really difficult to get any water out of them, so have a go if you're unsure. A cup that water flows easily out of is best for starters.

Babies don't need fruit juice and if you start offering it they may be reluctant to drink plain water, which is really the best drink, along with milk. If you want to give fruit juice, make sure it is 100% pure juice rather than a juice drink, which will contain sugar or artificial sweeteners and other additives. Juices should be diluted one part juice to 10 parts water. Babies shouldn't be given fizzy drinks as these can damage newly emerging teeth, nor tea or coffee as these contain caffeine and polyphenols, which interfere with iron absorption.

Supplements

The Department of Health recommends that from 6 months of age babies should be given a supplement containing vitamins A, C and D. This is unless babies are drinking at least 500ml of formula a day, as formula has the vitamins added to it.

If you are eligible for the government's Healthy Start scheme you can get vitamin drops for your baby free with a voucher. If not, you can buy Healthy Start vitamin drops or another brand of vitamins from most pharmacists, including high street shops such as Boots and Superdrug.

Foods to avoid

You should avoid giving your baby certain foods to reduce the risk of allergies, choking, food poisoning and environmental pollutants. If you start weaning before 6 months old, it is best to give fruit, vegetables and cereals such as baby rice. Introducing certain foods before this age can lead to problems with digestion and can increase the risk of allergies.

Foods to try only after 6 months

- Meat, poultry, fish and seafood
- Eggs
- Cows' milk and milk products such as cheese and yogurt
- Nuts and seeds
- Beans and pulses
- Foods containing gluten, including bread, pasta and rusks
- Citrus fruits

Foods to avoid for the first year

Food	Why it should be avoided
Honey	May contain bacteria that can cause infant botulism.
Salt	Babies' kidneys can't cope with it and babies get a taste for it.
Sugar (including syrups and concentrated juice)	It doesn't provide the nutrients babies need, damages developing teeth and encourages a sweet tooth.

Continued over page

Continued from overleaf

Food	Why it should be avoided
Whole nuts	May cause choking.
Low-fat dairy foods	Babies need the calories and the fat-soluble vitamins that full-fat milk, yogurt and cheese contain.
Foods high in saturated or trans fats	Foods such as butter and fatty meat and processed foods such as cheap sausages and cakes contain unhealthy fats that are associated with heart disease.
Very high-fibre foods	Can cause digestive discomfort and fill a baby up before she's eaten enough to meet her nutritional needs.
Uncooked or partially cooked eggs	Babies are more susceptible to salmonella.
Soft mould-ripened or blue cheeses	Babies are more susceptible to listeria, so it is best not to give cheeses such as brie, Danish blue or goats' cheese.
Raw shellfish	Can cause food poisoning.
Shark, swordfish and marlin	Contain mercury, which could affect the developing nervous system, therefore not recommended for under-16s.
Smoked and salted meats and fish	Contain salt and preservatives that have been linked to cancer risk.
Caffeine	It's a stimulant and can cause restlessness, increased heart rate and other problems.

Salt guidelines

- Babies under 1 year should have no more than 1g of salt per day (0.4g sodium).
- Toddlers between 1 and 3 years old should have no more than 2g of salt per day (0.8g sodium).

As well as avoiding adding salt when you're cooking and at the table, it's important to look out for salt in everyday food products such as bread and biscuits and try to swap these for lower salt alternatives. It's very easy for babies to go over the 1g limit, for example, if they eat one slice of bread for breakfast and have some gravy with their dinner.

High salt foods and healthier alternatives

High salt foods	Healthier alternatives with less than 0.1g salt
Bread (0.4–0.5g per slice)	Rice
	Pasta
	Couscous
Cornflakes (0.3g per 20g)	Oatibix
Digestive biscuit (0.2g per biscuit)	Rusk or homemade biscuit (p100)
Ham (0.4g per slice)	Roast chicken
Sausages (0.5–1.3g per sausage)	Roast or stewed pork
Bacon (0.7g per rasher)	
Smoked salmon (2.4g per 50g)	Grilled or baked salmon
Tomato ketchup (0.3g per tbsp)	Low salt tomato ketchup (p183)
Stock from a stock cube (0.4g per 50ml)	Stock from a very low salt stock cube
Gravy from granules (0.5g per 50ml)	Homemade gravy or sauce without salt

Preparing food for your baby

Cooking for babies is different to cooking just for adults as you have to be more careful about food hygiene. Babies are more susceptible to salmonella, listeria and other forms of food poisoning, so it's important to take some basic precautions. Also, as babies tend to eat more cooked food, rather than breakfast cereal, bread or raw fruit and salad, most parents end up doing more batch cooking and reheating. This needs to be done carefully to ensure that harmful bacteria don't get the opportunity to multiply and cause problems.

To protect your baby from food poisoning, make sure you follow these rules:

- Wash your hands.
- Wash all fruit and vegetables that you are going to give your baby. This is important even if you are going to peel or cook the food as bacteria can be transferred to the flesh or to hands and equipment such as chopping boards. This may seem overly cautious but in recent years food poisoning outbreaks have been traced back to watermelons, potatoes and leeks. Thorough washing is especially important for foods that are going to be eaten raw, such as avocado or mango.
- There is no need to sterilise equipment, but make sure you keep cooking utensils and work surfaces clean.
- Make sure that any food for your baby is within its 'Use by' or 'Best before' date.
- Keep your fridge clean, check the temperature is below 5°C and make sure foods are covered, particularly meat, fish and eggs. Keep your baby's food towards the back of the fridge where the temperature is more constant.
- When you're preparing a batch of food for the freezer, divide it into ice-cube trays or small pots as soon as possible, then it will cool more quickly. If you freeze purées in ice-cube trays you can later pop them into a freezer bag – but don't forget to label it clearly.
- Put cooked food into the fridge or freezer within an hour of cooking. For purées containing raw ingredients do this immediately.
- Defrost food in the fridge when possible. This is especially important for foods that are to be eaten raw, such as mango, to reduce the possibility of bacterial growth.

Using leftovers

Make use of leftovers whenever possible. You can even cook extra vegetables, baked potatoes, pasta and soup or casserole at normal mealtimes, so you have some to store. Just remember to get leftovers into the fridge or freezer as quickly as possible and follow the basic hygiene rules.

Feeding your baby

When you feed your baby it should be pleasant and relaxing for you both. However, there are a few simple precautions that you need to take in order to avoid the risks of food poisoning or choking.

- Wash your baby's hands.
- Only give your baby food when she is **sitting up**, either in a chair or on your lap, to avoid choking.
- Always **stay with your baby** when she's eating.
- When **reheating** food, make sure it is really hot in the centre, then leave it to cool before giving it to your baby. If it isn't eaten, throw it away, as it can't go back in the fridge or freezer. Never reheat food more than once.
- **Avoid choking hazards** such as small, hard pieces of food like whole nuts. Small, round foods such as grapes, blueberries and cherry tomatoes should be cut in half. Don't give raw apple or carrot until your baby is more experienced with food and then cut them into thin sticks or slices. Be guided by your baby when it comes to foods like this, as some cope much better than others. Also, when you give your baby fish, check that it doesn't contain any bones.
- **Know how to handle choking** in case it ever occurs. Make sure you know the difference between choking and gagging. Gagging is a safety mechanism and just the way babies bring food back to the front of their mouth to chew. Some babies gag fairly regularly as they learn how to cope with different foods and this isn't a problem. When a baby is choking she is usually unable to breathe or cry. To find out how to recognise what's happening and how to handle choking you can look at www.nhs.uk and www.babycentre.co.uk or you could go on a parenting course.

Allergies and food intolerances

Some foods are more likely to cause an allergic reaction than others and it is a good idea to introduce these foods one at a time. Foods least likely to cause a reaction should be given first (p24).

Foods that are most likely to cause an allergic reaction are:

- wheat
- peanuts and tree nuts (hazelnuts, walnuts, Brazil nuts)
- seeds (sesame, poppy)
- eggs
- cows' milk
- fish and shellfish.

Other foods that sometimes, but less often, cause allergies include celery, celeriac, soya, mustard, coconut, pine nuts and kiwi fruit. The general advice is to give only a small amount of these foods to start with, and only one at a time. Provided your baby doesn't show any reaction, she can then have them as a normal part of her diet along with other foods.

It is generally fairly easy to identify an allergy to a particular food as babies usually have an immediate reaction when they eat it, such as a rash, particularly around the mouth, or swelling, wheezing or vomiting. However, symptoms such as diarrhoea may occur a few hours after the food is eaten. A food intolerance is more common than an allergy, but symptoms of an intolerance are often more vague, making it more difficult to identify the trigger. A food intolerance can result in diarrhoea, eczema or a rash, or in a range of symptoms that can make babies miserable, such as joint pain, abdominal pain or a headache. If you suspect your baby is allergic or intolerant to a particular food, it is best to avoid the food until you are able to see a medical professional. In the meantime, it's a good idea to keep a diary of your baby's diet and any symptoms.

Portion sizes

Many parents want to know how much food they should be giving their baby. They worry that she is not eating enough or is having too much. In reality the right amount for one baby may be too much or not enough for another baby of exactly the same age. Babies have different requirements and varying appetites.

If your baby is generally happy, healthy and growing then be guided by her appetite. She may eat virtually nothing one day and much more the next, but that's because she's listening to her body, a skill that unfortunately most adults have lost but that you want her to continue to have.

If you offer three meals and two healthy snacks a day, your baby has the opportunity to get all the nutrients she needs. You should then leave it up to her to eat as much or as little as she wants. There is more advice about reluctant eaters on p60 and on babies who don't seem to know when to stop on p59.

Kitchen equipment

You don't need any special 'baby food making equipment' in order to cook and feed your baby good nutritious meals. However, it is essential to have some basic equipment:

- food processor (with blender jug attachment) or hand-held blender (the latter is better if you don't like washing up)
- chopping boards: one for fruit and vegetables and a separate one for raw meat and fish
- mixing bowl
- casserole dish that can go on the hob and also in the oven, preferably one with a lid otherwise you might need to cover it with foil sometimes
- saucepans with lids for cooking foods such as pasta, rice and soup
- deep-sided frying pan with lid
- small frying pan
- baking trays
- cake tins
- sharp knives, silicone pastry brush, silicone spatula, measuring spoons and grater.

Other non-essential but useful equipment includes a garlic crusher, potato peeler, potato masher and lemon squeezer.

For freezing baby food you need ice-cube trays and pots, freezer bags and a permanent marker pen.

Feeding equipment includes a high chair, bibs, and plastic feeding bowls and spoons. You might also want something to cover the floor, either a splash mat or an old towel.

Buying food

Some foods, such as fresh fish, are best bought when you're planning a particular meal, but other ingredients are used in a wide range of dishes, so it's good to have them ready in the cupboard. Below is a list of everyday ingredients that you might want to stock up on. Many of them are cheaper if you buy them in bulk. If you have a selection of these, and some fresh fruit and vegetables, you'll always be able to rustle up a healthy meal.

You'll notice that there aren't any jars, pots or pouches of baby food on the list, or any rusks or baby-friendly snacks. This is because they aren't really essential. The only special baby-friendly ingredient that really is different to regular products is very low salt stock cubes. Fruit purées made for babies are also good to have in the cupboard as they are very convenient, nutritionally sound and taste much like those you'd make yourself.

Store cupboard essentials

- Oats, Weetabix and other similar cereals
- Pasta, rice and couscous
- Plain flour (but self-raising, wholemeal and cornflour are also useful)
- Dry red lentils
- Tins of chopped tomatoes, passata and tomato purée
- Tins of beans and pulses such as chickpeas, butter beans and green lentils
- Tins of fish, including tuna, sardines and mackerel
- Very low salt stock cubes
- Spices, including coriander, cumin, sweet paprika, cinnamon and mixed spice
- Dried herbs, including bay leaves, parsley and basil
- Rapeseed oil and olive oil
- Greaseproof paper or baking parchment

Fridge and freezer essentials

- Natural yogurt
- Eggs
- Cheese, such as Cheddar, mozzarella, ricotta and cream cheese
- Houmous
- Frozen vegetables such as peas, green beans and spinach

Planning meals

Many of us end up cooking the same meals all the time and it's easy to end up doing the same for your baby, especially if you find something she really likes. However, if you try to vary what you cook, it can help ward off fussy eating. In each of the four sections of this book you'll find meal plans to help you see the kind of foods you should be offering your baby over a few days.

Happy cooking!

Cooking should be fun. Even if you don't find it exactly relaxing, it shouldn't be a chore. It's important to find what works for you and your baby, whether that means everyone eating exactly the same foods at every meal or only sharing the odd dish together. Ultimately you want to be able to cook one meal that everyone will eat, so it's important to find healthy foods that the whole family enjoys. It's also essential to find meals that you have time to cook and that don't involve overly expensive ingredients.

Don't be afraid to make up your own recipes or adapt recipes in this book or those you find elsewhere. For example, if you have lots of broccoli in the fridge, make broccoli fingers instead of courgette fingers (p73). Making up your own recipes can be fun, but be careful you're not adding cheese or breadcrumbs to everything. These may encourage babies to eat up and they're good for binding finger foods together, but they're also quite salty. Try eggs, oats and potato instead.

The recipes in this book are set out in ages, starting with some simple purées and finger foods and going through to more interesting dishes that the whole family will hopefully enjoy together. Broadly speaking, as you go through the book the dishes become increasingly adventurous and will suit those with more teeth and better co-ordination. If you find your baby is coping well with lumps, finger foods and stronger flavours, there's no reason at all why you can't choose recipes from a section for older babies. The way the recipes are arranged should be taken as only a rough guide. Likewise, as your baby progresses, there's no reason to stop serving foods from earlier chapters. The idea is to expand your baby's diet by introducing additional foods and dishes.

Author's recipe notes

- **Rapeseed oil**, also known as canola oil, is used in many of the recipes as it contains only 7% saturated fat, compared with 52% in butter and 14% in olive oil. It is also preferable to sunflower oil as it contains less omega 6 fatty acids, which interfere with omega 3 fatty acid metabolism. Olive oil is a good alternative and it is used in some recipes, partly for its flavour. Another consideration is that at high temperatures rapeseed oil is more stable than olive oil.
- Most recipes are suitable for **reheating** in a microwave and unless the instructions say otherwise it is fine to do this.

However, some, such as pancakes and fritters, are better reheated in the oven or under the grill, as they can't be stirred like a purée to ensure an even temperature throughout. Reheating in the microwave isn't dangerous but it spoils the texture and they can become a bit dry and rubbery.

- **Portion sizes** are given for each recipe but these are very rough estimates. Babies may start off by eating just one ice-cube-sized portion and quickly move on to two or three times as much. Meals suitable for the whole family give estimates for adults or adults and babies or children.
- An approximate **preparation time** is given for each recipe. For foods that need watching while they're cooking, the cooking time is simply included in this. If you can leave something cooking and get on with other things, then a separate cooking time is also given.
- Where **tablespoon** (tbsp) or **teaspoon** (tsp) quantities are given, these should be level, unless stated otherwise.
- If your baby has specific **dietary requirements**, many of the recipes in this book can be easily adapted. Substitutions can be made to milk by using lactose-free formula or soy milk; vegan or dairy-free margarine could be used instead of butter or margarine; gluten-free pasta or egg free pasta can be used instead of normal pasta. If your baby has a gluten intolerance, make sure you chose suitable stock cubes and baking po r.

Abbreviations used

°C – degrees centigrade

cm – centimetres

°F – degrees Fahrenheit

g – grams

ml – millilitres

mm – millimetres

tbsp – tablespoon (approx. 15g/15ml)

tsp – teaspoon (approx. 5g/5ml)

Conversion chart

We have used metric measurements throughout the book. Should you want to convert the measurements to imperial, here is a rough guide.

Metric	Imperial
Grams (g)	Ounces (oz)
25g	1oz
50g	2oz
100g	3½oz
150g	5oz
Millilitres (ml)	Fluid ounces (fl oz)
50ml	1¾fl oz
100ml	3½fl oz
150ml	5fl oz
Centimetres	Inches
2½cm	1 inch

2 Feeding your 4- to 6-month-old

When you feel your baby is ready for her first taste of food, the next step is to decide what to give her and how. If you're still unsure whether you'd rather start with a purée or some finger food you can always try both. For example, give your baby a steamed carrot baton to hold while you feed her a mashed-up piece. Whatever you choose, the most suitable meal for getting started is a little fruit, vegetable or baby rice. It is best to begin with something soft enough to chew or gum and easy to digest (see below). If your baby is 6 months old and is just starting to wean, it's good to begin with the same foods, but you can generally progress much faster than you would with a younger baby and start introducing other foods within a couple of weeks.

> ## Foods for absolute beginners
> - Carrot, butternut squash, sweet potato or parsnip: peeled and boiled, steamed or roasted, then given as batons or purée.
> - Broccoli or cauliflower: boiled or steamed and given as florets or purée.
> - Apple: peeled, cored and given as cooked wedges or purée.
> - Pear: peeled, cored and given raw (if very ripe), stewed or puréed.
>
> Some people choose to start with other foods, such as avocado or banana, but those listed here are probably the most common first foods.

Once babies are 6 months old and have tried a few simple foods they can start having a much more varied diet. At this age, solids become an increasingly important source of iron and other nutrients, as the stores babies were born with are beginning to run low. Milk is still needed for a while yet, but from this stage you can start to give your baby larger meals and more of them. By the time babies are 7 months old, they should be having three meals a day, as well as three or four milk feeds. Some will also have one or two snacks a day, but these aren't essential at this stage. You can also introduce a range of flavours and textures. If your baby has been having very smooth purées you can start to make these a little lumpier.

Babies who are 6 months old can start to have:

- protein foods such as meat, fish, beans and lentils
- well-cooked eggs
- foods containing wheat and gluten, including bread, pasta, Weetabix and oats
- full-fat dairy produce, including cheese and yogurt.

Purées

If you're going to start with purées you can either opt for baby rice mixed with a little of your baby's usual milk (breast or formula milk) or give a purée made from one of the fruits or vegetables mentioned above. The advantage of baby rice is that, mixed with milk, it tastes pretty much like the milk your baby is used to. However, if your baby is prone to constipation, it may be better to begin with pear as this is easier to digest and less likely to cause any problems. Most babies start with a fairly smooth, runny purée, which has a consistency similar to yogurt. However, if your baby is 6 months old or older, there isn't really a need for this – but it's still best to do whatever you feel most comfortable with. If you're concerned about choking, begin with a smooth purée and slowly move on to lumpier meals.

Finger foods

Whether you're starting with BLW or your baby has had some purées and is now ready to move on, it's important to choose nutritious finger foods. Suitable finger foods aren't just the things you buy in packets labelled as 'finger foods' but anything your baby can pick up, from broccoli florets to noodles. The kinds of foods that most babies start with are listed on p24.

It is best to give these as batons or chunks that are thick enough not to get mushed as soon as your baby grasps them. For foods such as carrots, try to make them long enough to stick out of your baby's fist. Plain unsalted and unflavoured rice cakes are another good food at the beginning, as they are easy to hold and can be gummed without turning mushy too quickly.

Breakfasts

Breakfast is usually the last meal to be added, once babies are in the habit of eating lunch and dinner every day. For babies under 6 months, the best breakfast is a little fruit purée with baby rice, or you can buy a gluten-free porridge.

From 6 months, babies can have Weetabix or similar cereals, or regular porridge made with their usual milk or full-fat cows' milk. There is also a range of fortified cereals available for babies this age. Get a plain version and give it to your baby with some fruit purée, chopped fruit or pieces she can feed herself. There are plenty of ideas for spicing up plain cereals on page 64.

If you'd rather give your baby something she can eat with her hands, then runny porridges aren't really appropriate until she is able to manage a spoon, but many BLW mums like porridge fingers. As these are made with about a third of the volume of milk that you would use to make a regular bowl of porridge, it's important your baby has plenty to drink with them. Pancakes are another breakfast for eating with your hands, and as well as the recipes below there are more pancake ideas on page 111.

Porridge fingers (6 months+)

These are basically just oats mixed with an equal volume of milk, then microwaved. Many BLWers rave about them but some find it takes a little experimenting to get them just right.

2 tbsp oats (not instant oat cereal, which is powdery, nor jumbo oats)
2 tbsp milk (cows' milk, breast milk or formula)

Preparation time: 5 minutes.
Equipment: 1 small microwaveable plate.
Storage: Best eaten straight away.

Servings: 1 for a 6-month-old baby. For older babies just add an extra spoonful or two of each ingredient.

- Mix the oats and milk together on the plate. Form the mixture into an approximate rectangle with the back of a spoon.
- Place in the microwave, uncovered, and cook for 1½ minutes. This is for a 900W microwave – it may take longer in lower wattage models.
- Leave for a few minutes to cool down and firm up, then cut into three toast soldier-sized pieces.

Tips

- The time they take to cook depends on your microwave and the dish you're cooking them in. If they turn out too sloppy or too rubbery to start with you just need to experiment.
- Try adding **dried fruit** such as sultanas, raisins, chopped apricot or chopped prune.
- To make **apple and cinnamon fingers,** grate a quarter of an apple into the mixture and add a pinch of cinnamon. After microwaving for 90 seconds, turn over with a fish slice and cook for an extra 30 seconds.
- For **banana porridge fingers,** add half a small mashed banana, cook for 90 seconds, turn over and cook for 30 more.

Polenta pancakes (6 months+)

These are surprisingly easy to make and very tasty. Use them instead of bread at breakfast or lunchtime to keep salt levels down.

> 2 eggs
> 300ml milk
> 125g polenta
> 1 tbsp rapeseed oil

Preparation time: 15–20 minutes.
Equipment: 1 large measuring jug and 1 frying pan.
Storage: Fridge for 1–2 days or freeze. Reheat in the oven or under the grill, as they go rubbery in the microwave.
Servings: 16 pancakes.

- Measure out 300ml of milk.
- Crack the eggs into the milk and beat well with a fork or wire whisk.

- Gradually add the polenta and beat until you have a smooth mixture.
- Heat a teaspoonful of oil in the frying pan and spoon two tablespoonfuls of mixture in for each pancake. You should be able to make four pancakes at a time.
- Cook for about 1 minute until the edges look cooked and bubbles can be seen on the surface. Then flip the pancakes over and cook for another minute on the other side.
- Heat another teaspoonful of oil in the frying pan before making the next batch and give the batter a good stir, as the polenta sinks to the bottom quite quickly.

Tips

- Serve for breakfast with pieces of fruit or purée.
- These are also good with a dip such as houmous, or just as they are with roast vegetables, pieces of chicken or just about anything.
- Try adding some grated cheese to the mixture.

Egg-free banana pancakes (6 months+)

These tasty pancakes are ideal if you're not ready to give your baby eggs yet or if she's had a reaction to eggs. They make a lovely breakfast with some sliced banana and a dollop of Greek yogurt.

1 medium ripe banana
125g plain flour
1 tsp baking powder
250ml milk
1 tbsp rapeseed oil

Preparation time: 15–20 minutes.
Equipment: 1 frying pan and 1 blender jug or hand-held blender with beaker.
Storage: Fridge for 1–2 days or freeze. Reheat in the oven or under the grill, as they go rubbery in the microwave.
Servings: 16 pancakes – enough for 2 adults and 1 baby.

- Whizz all the ingredients, except the oil, together in the blender.
- Heat a teaspoonful of the oil in the frying pan, then pour in about two tablespoonfuls of the mixture to make each pancake. You should be able to make three or four pancakes at a time.

- Once the edges of the pancake look dry, and bubbles have appeared all over, flip the pancake over. This takes only about 30 seconds.

Tips

- Try replacing half the flour with oats or using other flours, such as wholemeal or gluten-free flour.

Lunches and dinners

Lunch is usually the meal babies start having first, partly because any allergic reaction or other problem can be dealt with more easily during the daytime. Also, babies are often more alert and happy then, and there's more time available. To start with, planning a balanced meal is less important than getting your baby used to trying new foods. Some of the recipes here are for simple purées and finger foods, but there are also family recipes as it's never too soon to start sharing meals with your baby. When you eat together your baby can have the food in the same way as you, or you can purée, mash or chop your baby's portion.

Simple vegetable or fruit purée

The method for making a simple purée is basically the same for most fruits and vegetables. It's best to start by giving individual fruits and vegetables so your baby gets used to the idea that food doesn't always taste the same but has a range of flavours. Later you can give mixed purées.

> 500g of one of the following: carrots, parsnips, apples, sweet potato or butternut squash
> *or* one whole broccoli or cauliflower
> 100ml water

Preparation time: 25 minutes.
Equipment: 1 saucepan, 2 ice-cube trays for freezing and 1 food processor or hand-held blender.
Storage: Fridge for 1–2 days or freeze.
Servings: 28 ice-cube-sized pieces or about 14 baby meals.

- Wash the vegetables.
- Prepare the fruit or vegetables. For example, peel and core apples, peel carrots or other root vegetables or cut broccoli or cauliflower into small florets.

- Put the water in the pan and bring to the boil, then add the fruit or vegetable. Bring back to the boil and simmer for about 10 minutes until soft. Add a little more water if needed.
- Drain the cooking water into a small jug or cup. Mash or purée the fruit or vegetables either using a hand-held blender or in a food processor. Add as much of the cooking water as needed to make the purée the right consistency.
- Spoon the purée into the ice-cube trays so that it will cool down quickly.
- Once cool, put the ice-cube trays in a freezer bag or cover them with cling film and place in the freezer.
- Once frozen, you can pop the cubes into a labelled freezer bag and return them immediately to the freezer.

Tips

- When you are serving the purée you might want to add a little of your baby's usual milk (breast or formula milk) to make it runnier.
- To make potato purée, you'll need to cook it for a little longer – about 20 minutes – until it is nice and soft. Then mash the potato with a fork or potato masher rather than using a blender, as this can make it rather gluey.
- To make pear purée, cook over a low heat to start with and add only a tablespoon of water as pears produce quite a bit of liquid themselves and make a watery-looking purée. After puréeing you can add some baby rice to thicken it up.

Roasted butternut squash and red pepper purée

A simple purée with a smooth, creamy texture to introduce new vegetables.

1 large butternut squash
1 red pepper
2 bay leaves
1 tbsp olive or rapeseed oil

Preparation time: 20 minutes plus 20–25 minutes cooking.
Equipment: 2 baking trays or roasting tins and 1 food processor or hand-held blender.
Storage: Fridge for 1–2 days or freeze.
Servings: 10–12 baby portions.

- Put your roasting tins in the oven and preheat to 220°C/425°F/gas mark 7.
- Cut the squash in half lengthways and scoop out the seeds and membrane with a spoon and discard. Cut it into 1½cm thick slices, leaving the skin on.
- Brush or spray the slices with oil and arrange in one of the roasting tins, with the bay leaves.
- Cut the pepper into quarters and discard the seeds and membrane.
- Brush or spray the pepper with oil and place the quarters on a piece of foil in the other roasting tin.
- Leave to cook for 20–25 minutes, turning halfway through.
- Remove from the oven and close the foil around the pepper (this makes it easier to remove the skin).
- When the squash and peppers are cool enough to handle, remove the skin and then purée the vegetables with a blender. If needed, add some water or your baby's usual milk to thin the mixture.

Tips

- This has quite a strong flavour and some babies may prefer it mixed with potato or baby rice.

66 *Olivia has a sweet tooth and is less impressed by vegetables but really enjoyed this. It was much sweeter than expected and easier to make. I also served it with carrot, which got consumed very quickly too, so it's a winner.* 99
Charlie, mum to Sophie, 3 years, and Olivia, 6 months

Sweet potato and avocado

A lovely, creamy dish packed with beta-carotene for eye development, potassium for muscle function and healthy monounsaturated fats.

½ small sweet potato
½ small avocado
1–2 tbsp water or your baby's usual milk (breast or formula)

Preparation time: 10 minutes.
Equipment: 1 bowl and 1 hand-held blender (optional).
Storage: Fridge for 24 hours, or freeze for up to 2 weeks (freezing for longer may affect the colour and texture of the avocado) then defrost in the fridge.
Servings: 2–3 baby portions.

- Scrub the sweet potato and place in the microwave for about 5 minutes until cooked.
- Cut the sweet potato in half and scoop out the middle into a bowl.
- Cut the avocado in half and remove the stone. Scoop the flesh out of one half and add it to the sweet potato.
- Add the water (or milk) and mash with a fork or purée with a blender.

Tips

- If you're making this for a baby older than 6 months you can use cows' milk.

> ❝ I would never have thought to add avocado to sweet potato, but my little one seemed to really enjoy this! ❞
> **Nikki, mum to Connor, 5½ months**

Cauliflower, potato and chive mash

This is one to try after simple purées of carrot or apple. It can be puréed for younger babies or just mashed for older ones.

½ medium cauliflower
1 large potato
150ml water
1–2 tsp chopped chives (optional)
2 tbsp baby's usual milk (breast or formula)

Preparation time: 25 minutes.
Equipment: 1 saucepan.
Storage: Fridge for 1–2 days or freeze.
Servings: 8–10 baby portions.

- Peel and dice the potatoes into about 1cm cubes.
- Place the potato cubes in the pan with 150ml of water. Bring to the boil and simmer for 5 minutes.
- Meanwhile, chop the cauliflower into pieces about the same size as the potato.
- When the potatoes have cooked for 5 minutes, add the cauliflower to the pan, on top of the potato so it's just steaming rather than boiling.
- If you're using chives, snip these into the pan. This is easier to do with scissors rather than with a knife.

- When the cauliflower has been steaming for 5 minutes, give the pan a stir and cook for about 5 minutes more until both the potato and the cauliflower are tender.
- Add the milk and mash or purée the mixture, including the cooking water.

Tips

- If your baby is 6 months old, you can use cows' milk and add a little grated cheese to the dish.

Courgette, parsnip and pea purée

This is a sweet and creamy purée with a vivid green, flecked appearance.

2 medium parsnips
2 small courgettes
100ml water
75g frozen peas
baby's usual milk or water (optional)

Preparation time: 15–20 minutes.
Equipment: 1 saucepan.
Storage: Fridge for 1–2 days or freeze.
Servings: 10 baby portions.

- Peel the parsnips and cut them into 1cm cubes.
- Cut the ends off the courgettes, slice them in half lengthways and then slice quite thinly. They don't need to be peeled.
- Bring the parsnip and courgette to the boil with 100ml water, and simmer with the lid on for 5 minutes.
- Add the peas to the pan, bring back to the boil and simmer for 5 minutes more until the vegetables are tender.
- Purée the vegetables with the cooking water.
- Add a little extra water or some of your baby's usual milk (breast or formula) to thin the purée if needed.

Spinach, pea and potato purée

Spinach has quite a strong flavour for babies so a good way to introduce it is mixed with peas, which are sweeter.

1 large potato
100g frozen spinach
100g frozen peas
50ml milk (either breast, formula or cows' milk if your baby is over 6 months)

Preparation time: 20–25 minutes.
Equipment: 1 saucepan, 1 microwaveable bowl, 1 food processor (optional) and ice-cube trays.
Storage: Fridge for 1–2 days or freeze.
Servings: 5–6 baby meals or 18–20 ice-cube-sized portions.

- Peel the potato, cut it into small cubes, and place them in the pan with enough water to cover. Then bring to the boil and simmer for 5–10 minutes until soft.
- Put the frozen spinach in the bowl and microwave for 3–4 minutes until warm.
- Add the frozen peas and microwave for a further 1½–2 minutes until cooked.
- Purée the vegetables in the bowl or transfer to a blender.
- Drain the potatoes, add the milk and mash until smooth.
- Mix the vegetables with the mashed potato and spoon into ice-cube trays or containers.

Tips

- Serve with a high vitamin C dessert, such as apple and mango purée or mashed strawberries. This will increase the amount of iron that can be absorbed from the meal.
- Mixing some mashed avocado into this dish before serving makes it taste creamier and adds vitamin C and monounsaturated fatty acids.
- Babies over 6 months can have some grated cheese mixed in.

More ideas for mixed vegetable purées
- Carrot and potato
- Carrot and swede
- Carrot and cauliflower
- Carrot, swede and parsnip
- Cauliflower, broccoli and potato
- Leek, pea and potato

- Courgette and sweet potato
- Butternut squash and carrot
- Avocado and potato
- Carrot, potato and butternut squash

Steamed or boiled vegetable sticks

Root vegetables can all be prepared in the same way really, although some will take longer to cook than others.

Any of the following:
carrots, parsnips, sweet potatoes

Preparation time: 20 minutes.
Equipment: 1 saucepan or steamer.
Storage: Fridge for 24 hours or freeze.
Servings: A medium carrot will make 6–8 sticks or batons.

- Wash and peel the vegetables. Cut them into chunky chip shapes.
- Steam the vegetables if you have a steamer.
- If not, place about 1cm of water in a pan and put the lid on. Bring to the boil then add the vegetables and simmer until tender.

Tips

- Add a little more water if needed so that the pan doesn't boil dry, but B vitamins and vitamin C are easily leached out so add as little as possible.
- If parsnips are a bit stringy in the centre, remove this section.
- To prepare broccoli or cauliflower, cut into florets and prepare as above.
- Green beans and baby sweetcorn can be cooked the same way.

Roast carrot and parsnip fingers

Roasting vegetables makes a nice change to boiling or steaming. It takes a little longer but gives the vegetables a sweeter taste and you can make a batch for freezing or for feeding the whole family.

1 medium carrot
1 medium parsnip
1 tsp olive oil

Preparation time: 5 minutes plus 20 minutes cooking.
Equipment: 1 baking tray.
Storage: Best eaten fresh. Can store in the fridge for 1–2 days or freeze. Reheat in the microwave or, if you want them firmer, in the oven or under the grill.
Servings: 2 baby portions.

- Preheat the oven to 220°C/425°F/gas mark 7.
- Peel the vegetables and cut off the ends.
- Cut the vegetables in half lengthways, and if necessary cut them in half widthways too. The thick end of large carrots and parsnips can be cut into quarters but don't make the sticks too thin, as they'll shrink when they're cooked.
- Put the vegetable fingers in a food bag, add the oil and toss to cover, or brush them with the oil.
- Place them on a baking tray and roast them in the oven for 20 minutes, turning occasionally.

Tips

- You can cook these with thick strips of red pepper, courgette and sweet potato to make a really colourful vegetable mixture for everyone to share.

Roasted butternut squash with ginger

This is a great flavour combination. The way it's cooked means you get a hint of ginger without it being overpowering.

1 butternut squash
2½cm fresh ginger
2 bay leaves
1–2 tsp olive or rapeseed oil

Preparation time: 10 minutes plus 20–30 minutes cooking.
Equipment: 1 roasting tin.
Storage: Fridge for 1–2 days or freeze.
Servings: 6–8 baby portions.

- Preheat the oven to 220°C/425°F/gas mark 7.
- Cut the squash in half lengthways and scoop out the seeds and membrane with a spoon. Cut it into 1½cm thick slices, leaving the skin on.

- Brush the slices with oil and arrange in a roasting tin.
- Remove the skin from the ginger and cut it into about eight pieces. These can be bashed or squashed a bit but not grated, as you want to be able to remove them later.
- Scatter the pieces of ginger and the bay leaves into the tin and cook for 20–30 minutes, turning the squash halfway through.
- Remove from the oven and leave to cool.

Tips

- You can remove the skin from the slices if you wish or leave it on. Some babies find it easier to handle with the skin left on.

Baked asparagus

This is a great finger food for babies and adults alike.

1 bunch of asparagus (about 175g)
1 tsp olive oil
1 tsp lemon juice

Preparation time: 5 minutes plus 10–15 minutes cooking.
Equipment: 1 baking tray.
Storage: Fridge for 1–2 days.
Servings: 2 adults and 1 baby.

- Preheat the oven to 180°C/350°F/gas mark 4.
- Place a piece of foil on the baking tray and arrange the asparagus in a single layer in the centre.
- Drizzle over the oil and lemon juice.
- Wrap the foil snugly but not too tightly around the asparagus and seal the edges by folding them together tightly.
- Bake for 10–15 minutes.
- Remove from the oven and serve warm or cold.

Roast cauliflower

This is a good way of introducing the distinct flavour of cauliflower, and it may even convert cauliflower sceptics in the family.

> 1 medium cauliflower
> 1–2 tsp olive or rapeseed oil
> 2 cloves garlic, crushed (optional)
> 2 bay leaves (optional)
> juice of ½ lemon (optional)

Preparation time: 10 minutes plus 30 minutes cooking.
Equipment: 1 roasting tin.
Storage: Fridge for 1–2 days or freeze. Reheat in the microwave or oven.
Servings: 4 adults or 15–20 baby portions.

- Preheat the oven to 220°C/425°F/gas mark 7.
- Remove the outer leaves of the cauliflower then rinse and cut it into florets.
- Brush the florets with oil, or spray, and put them in a single layer in the roasting tin. Add the optional extras.
- Roast for 30 minutes.
- Remove from the oven and serve warm or cold.

Tips

- These can be eaten as they are, dipped in houmous or with a bit of grated cheese on top (providing your baby is over 6 months old).

Basic tomato sauce (6 months+)

This sauce may turn into your go-to recipe over the next year. It forms the basis of many meals, even something as quick and simple as pasta, sauce and cheese, and you can feel confident in the knowledge that your little one is getting lots of vegetables all at once.

> 1 red onion
> 2 × 400g tins chopped tomatoes
> 2 cloves garlic, crushed
> 3 medium carrots
> 1 red pepper
> ½ head of broccoli
> 1 tbsp tomato purée
> some fresh basil or 1 tsp dried basil
> 1 tbsp olive oil

Preparation time: 20 minutes plus 30 minutes cooking.
Equipment: 1 large saucepan with lid and 1 food processor or hand-held blender.
Storage: Fridge for 1–2 days or freeze.
Servings: 10–15 portions to use as part of a meal.

- Finely chop the onion, carrots and pepper.
- Sweat the onion for a few minutes in the olive oil. Add the chopped carrots and red pepper and leave to cook, with the lid partly covering the pan, for about 10 minutes. Stir occasionally.
- Add the garlic and stir well.
- Pour in the chopped tomatoes and stir in the purée, broccoli and two tins of water (use the empty tomato tin). Add the basil.
- Simmer for about 30 minutes or until all the vegetables are really soft. Blend well, to create a smooth consistency.

Tagliatelle with green sauce (6 months+)

This smooth and creamy broccoli and courgette sauce is quick and easy to prepare and even the most broccoli-phobic will enjoy it. Babies can have the whole dish puréed or leave the tagliatelle whole – the sauce clings well to the pasta for self-feeding.

1 onion
2 cloves garlic, crushed
3 mushrooms
1 tbsp olive oil
½ head of broccoli
1 medium courgette
½ very low salt stock cube mixed with 100ml water
2 tsp mixed herbs
3 tbsp cream cheese
black pepper
tagliatelle

Preparation time: 25 minutes.
Equipment: 1 deep frying pan, 1 large saucepan and 1 food processor or hand-held blender.
Storage: Fridge for 1–2 days or freeze.
Servings: 2 adults and 1 baby.

- Cook the tagliatelle according to the instructions on the pack.
- Dice the onion and slice the mushrooms.
- Heat the oil in the frying pan and sauté the onion, mushrooms and crushed garlic for a few minutes.
- Cut the courgette in quarters lengthways and slice, then add to the pan.
- Chop the broccoli into small pieces and cook with the other ingredients for another 5 minutes, stirring occasionally.
- Add the stock and mixed herbs and cook for another 5 minutes with the lid on until the vegetables are soft. Add a little extra water if needed.
- Stir in the cream cheese and black pepper and warm through. Then blend until smooth, mix with the tagliatelle and serve.

Tips

- For adults, and older babies with a few teeth, sprinkle some toasted pine nuts on top.

Red pepper and polenta soldiers (6 months+)

If you've never tried polenta before then you'll be pleasantly surprised at how easy these are to prepare. And if you've tried it before and found it bland, you'll be amazed at how tasty they are.

1 tsp olive oil
½ red pepper
½ × 400g tin chopped tomatoes
1 tbsp tomato purée
1 tbsp chopped fresh basil or 1 tsp dried basil
100g polenta
1 very low salt stock cube made up with 400ml boiling water
50g Cheddar cheese

Preparation time: 30 minutes plus 1 hour cooling and 10 minutes grilling.
Equipment: 1 small frying pan, 1 saucepan and 1 baking tray.
Storage: Fridge for 1–2 days or freeze before grilling.
Servings: 26 fingers.

- Finely dice the red pepper and chop the basil.
- Heat the oil in the frying pan and cook the pepper until soft.
- Meanwhile grate the cheese and brush oil over the baking tray.
- Add the tomato, tomato purée and basil and cook for a few minutes then set aside.
- Put the stock in a pan and bring to the boil. Slowly pour the polenta into the pan, stirring all the time. Continue stirring for 2–3 minutes while the polenta thickens.
- Take the polenta off the heat then stir in the vegetable mixture and the cheese.
- Spoon the polenta onto the baking tray and, starting at one end, spread the mixture out so that it is about 1cm thick. You probably won't fill the whole baking tray but it is easy to make a straight line with the mixture at whatever point you get to.
- Let the mixture cool down for about 15 minutes then cover it with cling film and place in the fridge for about 45 minutes until set. It's fine if you leave it longer.
- Cut the polenta into toast soldier-shaped pieces. You can now put some of the pieces into the freezer in a bag or airtight container with greaseproof paper to separate the layers.
- Take the soldiers that are going to be eaten and brush with oil then grill for 5 minutes on each side.

Tips

- Experiment by trying other vegetables such as mushrooms, broccoli or butternut squash.

> 66 *Marcus hadn't had red pepper, tomatoes or cheese before and clearly liked the taste straight away. The good thing was he could eat at his own pace and didn't make half as much mess as usual. I look forward to trying variations with other flavours soon.* 99
> **Nick, dad to Marcus, 6 months**

Couscous patties (6 months+)

These are a good alternative to rice balls, which can go hard or dry on the outside if they're not coated in breadcrumbs. Not including breadcrumbs means a much lower salt content.

175g couscous
4 tsp rapeseed oil
1 onion
1 garlic clove, crushed
1 medium carrot
1 medium courgette
½ tsp ground coriander
½ tsp ground cumin
¼ lemon
100g yogurt
1 egg

Preparation time: 20 minutes plus 15 minutes in the fridge (or longer if you like) and 10 minutes cooking.
Equipment: 1 mixing bowl and 1 frying pan.
Storage: Fridge for 1–2 days or freeze. Reheat under the grill or in the oven.
Servings: 10 quarter pounder-sized patties or 20–25 small patties.

- Place the couscous in a mixing bowl with 225ml of boiling water and leave to one side.
- Peel and dice the onion.
- Heat two teaspoons of oil in the frying pan and start frying the onion with the crushed garlic.
- Peel and grate the carrot and add to the pan.
- Grate the courgette and add to the pan. Cook for 8–10 minutes until soft.
- Lightly beat the egg in a small cup.
- Add the spices and stir, then take off the heat.
- Fluff up the couscous with a fork then stir in the cooked vegetables, yogurt, egg and the juice and zest of the quarter of a lemon.
- Wet your hands, then take a ping-pong ball-sized piece of the mixture, form it into a ball, then flatten into a patty. Place the patties on a plate, cover with cling film and place in the fridge for 15 minutes. You can leave them for a few hours if that is more convenient.
- Heat two teaspoons of oil in the frying pan and cook the patties for 5 minutes on each side until nicely browned. Smaller patties will cook slightly more quickly.

Tips

- To make a well-balanced meal, these could be eaten with some ordinary houmous or soya bean and pea houmous (p69) and some extra vegetables or fruit.

Avocado and yogurt dip (6 months+)

A very quick dip that younger babies might like on its own and older ones can eat with corn flatbread, vegetable sticks or mixed with leftover pasta. Babies who don't like pieces of avocado sometimes go for this as it doesn't have the same texture, although it still has all the nutritional benefits.

1 medium avocado
100g natural yogurt
½–1 garlic clove, crushed (optional)
2 tsp lemon juice
pinch of paprika

Preparation time: 10 minutes.
Equipment: 1 bowl and 1 hand-held blender (optional).
Storage: Best eaten straight away or fridge for 24 hours.
Servings: 1 small bowl.

- Cut the avocado in half, scoop out the flesh and mash with a fork (if you want it really smooth you can use a blender).
- Add all the other ingredients and mix well.

Tips

- Raw garlic isn't for everyone. If you're giving this as a purée it's probably best to leave it out. If making a dip, maybe try just half a clove to start with.

66 *This was absolutely delicious freshly made. Ailsa enjoyed it and I had it with pitta for lunch too.* 99
Emma, mum to Rory, 3 years, and Ailsa, 6 months

Bean purée (6 months+)

This recipe uses flageolet beans, which aren't often eaten here but are popular in France and ideal for babies as they have a delicate flavour and are more tender than other beans such as kidney or haricot. This simple purée is very thick and is ideal for mixing with any vegetables to add some extra calories and protein.

> 1 tbsp olive oil
> 1 × 400g tin flageolet beans (in water)
> 1 garlic clove, crushed
> 1 tbsp fresh parsley, chopped, or ½ tsp dried parsley

Preparation time: 15 minutes.
Equipment: 1 saucepan and 1 food processor or hand-held blender.
Storage: Fridge for 1–2 days or freeze.
Servings: 12–14 ice-cube-sized portions. Mix 1 or 2 with vegetables for a meal.

- Heat the oil in the pan.
- Drain the beans and add to the pan. There will still be some water, which is fine.
- Add the crushed garlic and the parsley and stir.
- Bring to the boil and simmer for 3–4 minutes, stirring occasionally.
- Purée in a blender and divide into portions.

Tips

- Instead of flageolet beans you can try adzuki or butter beans.
- This is a handy dish to freeze in ice-cube trays. When you have leftover vegetables or if you're eating something that isn't appropriate for your baby, such as sausages, she can have this instead.

Yellow split pea dhal (6 months+)

This mild dhal is a good introduction to lentils and spices, and it can be eaten with vegetables or chapatti. Older babies and adults can have it as a side dish with chicken or vegetable curry and rice.

> 1 tbsp olive or rapeseed oil
> 1 onion
> 1 garlic clove, crushed
> 2½cm fresh ginger, grated
> ½ tsp turmeric
> ½ tsp ground cumin
> ½ tsp ground cinnamon

250g yellow split peas
1 bay leaf
750ml water
25g creamed coconut block (or 100ml creamed coconut)
juice of ¼ lemon

Preparation time: 15 minutes plus 45 minutes cooking.
Equipment: 1 saucepan.
Storage: Fridge for 1–2 days or freeze.
Servings: 2 adult and 1 baby or 10–12 baby portions.

- Finely dice the onion and fry in the oil for 2–3 minutes, along with the crushed garlic and grated ginger.
- Stir in the spices and cook for another minute.
- Add the split peas, bay leaf and water and stir well to make sure nothing is stuck to the bottom of the pan.
- Turn the heat up and bring to the boil, then turn it down, put the lid on and simmer for 40 minutes.
- Grate the creamed coconut into the pan, add the lemon juice and cook for a few more minutes.

Tips

- This can be puréed slightly if needed.
- Babies may like it mixed with other purées such as carrot or butternut squash and red pepper.
- Adults may like to add a little salt and pepper to taste.

Scrambled eggs (6 months+)

This is probably the easiest and quickest way to prepare eggs and a good way of introducing them to your baby.

1 egg
1 tbsp milk, yogurt or crème fraîche
1 tsp rapeseed oil, margarine or butter

Preparation time: 5 minutes.
Equipment: 1 small non-stick saucepan or frying pan.
Storage: Best eaten straight away.
Servings: 1 baby portion.

- Beat the egg and milk in a small cup.
- Heat the oil in the pan then add the egg mixture.
- Stir for 2–3 minutes until cooked.

Tips

- Scrambled eggs can be mixed with a few vegetables such as mushrooms or tomato. Simply fry these in the oil before adding the eggs to the pan.

Haddock and sweet potato (6 months+)

White fish is a good protein food for babies when they're just getting started as it's easy to digest and has a mild flavour.

1 medium sweet potato
1 haddock fillet (or other firm white fish such as sea bass, river cobbler or cod)
½ tsp olive oil
1 tsp fresh flat leaf parsley
1 squeeze of lemon

Preparation time: 20 minutes.
Equipment: 1 saucepan.
Storage: Fridge for 1–2 days or freeze.
Servings: 3–4 baby portions.

- Peel the sweet potato and chop into small pieces. Place in the pan with enough water to cover. Bring to the boil and simmer for 10–15 minutes until soft.
- Put the fish on a sheet of foil and drizzle over the oil and lemon juice. Grill for about 10 minutes, turning once.
- Finely chop the parsley.
- When the fish is cooked, flake the fish and check for bones.
- Drain the sweet potato (keeping some of the cooking water), add the parsley, fish and fish juices and mash with a fork. Add some of the cooking water if needed.

Tips

- If you have fish with skin on, grill it skin side up to start with, then turn over and add the oil and lemon. Then flake the fish off the skin after cooking.
- This dish can be puréed for younger babies.

- If you have leftover vegetables, such as carrots or broccoli, your baby can have these as finger food with the dish or they can be mixed in.
- If your baby is not keen on fish to start with, mix it with popular vegetables until she gets more used to it.

> 66 *This is easy to make and fantastic. It's the first time Kitty's had fish and she loved it.* 99
> **Charlotte, mum to Kitty, 6 months**

Chicken and vegetable purée (6 months+)

This simple purée is a good introduction to chicken as it is mixed with familiar vegetables.

3 broccoli florets
1 medium carrot
1 large parsnip
100ml water
1 tsp olive oil
100g chicken thigh

Preparation time: 30 minutes.
Equipment: 1 saucepan and 1 small frying pan.
Storage: Fridge for 1–2 days or freeze.
Servings: 5 baby portions.

- Peel and dice the carrot and parsnip and place in the pan with 100ml of water.
- Bring to the boil, put the lid on and simmer for 5 minutes.
- Chop the broccoli into small pieces and mix in with the other vegetables. Cook for 5 more minutes.
- Meanwhile cut the chicken into 1cm cubes. Heat the oil in the frying pan and cook the chicken for 4–5 minutes until browned.
- Add the chicken and any juices to the vegetables and cook on a low heat for another 5–10 minutes until all the vegetables are soft.
- Remove from the heat and purée according to your baby's needs. Divide into individual portions for freezing.

Tips

- You may want to make the purée runnier by adding a little milk or water.
- If your baby enjoys this simple purée you can try it with other vegetables and add a bay leaf and a pinch of mixed herbs for extra flavour.
- You can start by giving this purée as it is, but to make a well-balanced meal your baby needs to have it with something starchy such as rice or mashed potato.

> 66 *I made the purée and then used half to make chicken and vegetable fingers [below]. Kitty loved the purée and tried the sticks but didn't manage to eat much. I'll definitely make them again, though, when she's a bit more adept at finger foods and chewing.* 99
> **Charlotte, mum to Kitty, 6 months**

Chicken and vegetable fingers (6 months+)

The purée above can be turned into fingers for babies who want to feed themselves. This is also a good idea for encouraging babies to move on from having only purées.

You'll need all the ingredients listed above plus:
50g oats (not jumbo oats)
1 tsp rapeseed oil

Preparation time: 35 minutes plus 15–20 minutes cooking.
Equipment: 1 saucepan, 1 small frying pan (as above) and 1 baking tray.
Storage: Fridge for 1–2 days or freeze.
Servings: 5 baby portions.

- Prepare the chicken and vegetables as above and purée until coarsely chopped, or smoother if necessary.
- Preheat the oven to 200°C/400°F/gas mark 6.
- Brush the oil over the baking tray.
- Mix the oats with the purée. Take walnut-sized pieces of the mixture and shape them into thin sausages. Place on the baking tray.
- Bake for 15–20 minutes, turning occasionally, until browned.

Tips

- Freeze in a bag or airtight container with pieces of greaseproof paper between layers. They can either be frozen before cooking, then defrosted and cooked as described, or they can be frozen after cooking and reheated either in an oven for 5–10 minutes or under the grill.

Baby beef stew (6 months+)

Beef is one of the best sources of iron available and this warming stew is a good way of introducing it.

1 tsp olive oil
75g extra lean minced beef
1 medium potato
2 medium carrots
1 bay leaf
200ml water
25g frozen peas

Preparation time: 15 minutes plus 15 minutes cooking.
Equipment: 1 saucepan.
Storage: Fridge for 1–2 days or freeze.
Servings: 4–5 baby portions.

- Peel and dice the potatoes and carrots into 1–2cm pieces.
- Heat the oil in the pan. Add the mince and cook, stirring, until browned.
- Stir in the potato and carrot, then add the bay leaf and water.
- Bring to the boil, then simmer gently for 10–12 minutes until the vegetables are soft.
- Add the peas and simmer for 1–2 minutes.
- Pour the cooking water into a cup or jug and set aside. Then mash or purée the mixture, adding as much of the cooking juices as necessary to make a good consistency.

Tips

- Try adding a pinch of mixed herbs or a teaspoon of tomato purée to give the stew more flavour.

Pork and apple with rice (6 months+)

Pork and apple are a classic combination and they are combined here to make a purée that can be eaten with other vegetables or as a meal by itself.

50g rice (any kind)
1 tsp rapeseed oil
100g lean minced pork
½ medium apple
50g green or savoy cabbage
75ml water
1 bay leaf

Preparation time: 15 minutes plus 10–15 minutes cooking.
Equipment: 2 saucepans.
Storage: Fridge for 1–2 days or freeze.
Servings: 4–5 baby portions.

- Cook the rice according to the instructions on the pack.
- Peel, core and dice the apple and shred the cabbage.
- Heat the oil in the pan and cook the pork until browned.
- Add the apple, cabbage, water and bay leaf. Bring to the boil and simmer gently with the lid on for 10–15 minutes until tender.
- Add the cooked rice and purée to a consistency that suits your baby.

Tips

- Some babies like this mixed with their favourite vegetables, such as carrot, parsnip or peas.

Puddings and snacks

To start with, the best puddings are just fruit and it's up to you whether you offer your baby something sweet after both lunch and dinner every day or just sometimes. Some parents choose not to, as they're worried this could encourage a sweet tooth, and babies might decide to skip savoury foods in anticipation of something sweeter. This theory hasn't been tested but it's an idea you might want to consider.

Apple and mango purée

Wait until your mango is really ripe before making this, then it will be beautifully sweet and juicy as well as bursting with vitamin C.

4 medium eating apples
1 ripe mango
50ml water

Preparation time: 20 minutes.
Equipment: 1 saucepan and 1 hand-held blender.
Storage: Fridge for 24 hours or freeze immediately.
Servings: 6–8 baby portions.

- Cut the apples into quarters, remove the peel and core and cut into chunks.
- Place the apple in a pan with about 50ml of water and bring to the boil, then simmer gently for 5 minutes with the lid on, until soft. Stir occasionally and add extra water if needed so that the pan doesn't boil dry.
- Leave the apple to cool with the lid off.
- Cut the mango in half lengthways, as close to the stone as possible.
- Cut the mango into cubes, flesh side up, being careful not to cut through the skin. This will create a hedgehog effect and you can then cut the cubes off the skin.
- Add the mango to the cooled apple and use a hand-held blender to make the fruit as smooth as your baby needs. For older babies, just a few pulses with the blender should be enough.

Tips

- Be especially careful with food hygiene as not everything is cooked (p16).
- Babies over 6 months can have this mixed with natural yogurt or fromage frais.

> ❝ *I'm fascinated that Olivia liked mango – I think it has quite an "aromatic" taste and I thought it would be too complex for her, but she loved this.* ❞
> **Charlie, mum to Sophie, 3 years, and Olivia, 6 months**

Banana and blueberry purée

Blueberries are packed with antioxidants, including anthocyanins, which give them their wonderful colour.

80g blueberries (fresh or frozen)
1 small banana
1–2 tsp baby rice (optional)

Preparation time: 5 minutes.
Equipment: 1 hand-held blender with beaker.
Storage: Fridge for 24 hours.
Servings: 2–3 baby portions.

- Weigh the blueberries into the beaker or mug and add the banana, broken into pieces.
- Blend to the desired consistency.
- If the mixture is too runny, mix in some baby rice to thicken it.
- Put half the mixture into a baby bowl and leave the other half in the mug, covered with cling film, ready for tomorrow.

Tips

- Frozen blueberries are cheaper than fresh and have been found to contain the same levels of antioxidants. You don't need to defrost them completely before you start, but if they're rock solid they might shoot off when you start blending.

66 *I like this because it's really quick and now I have blueberries in the freezer I can make it again easily. I wasn't sure how Olivia would deal with the slightly gritty texture as we're only three weeks into weaning, but she absolutely loved it. I'll try adding it to natural yogurt when she's a bit bigger.* 99
Charlie, mum to Sophie, 3 years, and Olivia, 6 months

Pear and sultana purée

Cooked pear can be very runny but by combining it with dried fruit you get a thicker purée and extra iron.

3 ripe pears
3 tbsp sultanas

Preparation time: 15 minutes.
Equipment: 1 saucepan.
Storage: Fridge for 1–2 days or freeze.
Servings: 5–10 baby portions.

- Cut the pears into quarters, peel and core them, and cut them into chunks.
- Place the pear in the pan with just a tablespoon of water so that it doesn't stick to the bottom, and put it on a low heat with the lid on.
- After about 5 minutes, when you have 1cm of liquid at the bottom of the pan, add the sultanas, turn up the heat a bit and put the lid back on.
- Cook for 4–5 minutes longer until the sultanas have plumped up and the pear is tender.
- Purée to a suitable consistency.

Apple, apricot and banana purée

This is sweeter than plain apple purée and provides extra iron and beta-carotene.

2 medium eating apples
8 dried apricots
½ medium ripe banana

Preparation time: 15 minutes.
Equipment: 1 saucepan.
Storage: Fridge for 1–2 days or freeze.
Servings: 5–10 baby portions.

- Cut the apples into quarters, remove the peel and core, and cut them into chunks.
- Place the apple and apricots in a pan with about 75ml of water and bring to the boil, then simmer gently for 5 minutes with the lid on. Stir occasionally and add extra water if needed so that the pan doesn't boil dry.
- Slice the banana into the pan and cook for another 4–5 minutes.
- Mash or purée the fruit to a suitable consistency.

> 66 *I really like this fruit purée! It's much more interesting than just banana or apple. My baby was very keen on this one.* 99
> **Nikki, mum to Connor, 5½ months**

More ideas for mixed fruit purées

- Apple and dried apricot
- Apple and blueberry
- Apple and pear
- Banana and watermelon
- Banana and peach

Apple and squash dessert (6 months+)

This sounds like an odd combination but the flavours complement each other well and make a nutritious and not overly sweet dessert.

¼ medium butternut squash (about 100g)
100ml apple juice or water
1 medium eating apple
3 dates
pinch of cinnamon
full-fat natural yogurt (optional)

Preparation time: 10 minutes plus 15 minutes cooking.
Equipment: 1 saucepan.
Storage: Fridge for 1–2 days or freeze before adding the yogurt.
Servings: 6 baby portions.

- Peel the squash, cut it into 1cm cubes and place them in the pan with the apple juice or water. Cover, bring to the boil and simmer for 5 minutes.
- Peel and core the apple and cut it into chunks.
- Cut the dates in half and remove the stones.
- Add the apple, dates and cinnamon to the pan, bring back to the boil and simmer for 10 more minutes until everything is soft. Add extra water if necessary.
- Take off the heat, then purée the mixture to make it smooth enough to suit your baby.
- Mix one portion (warm or cold) with yogurt and serve.

> 66 *This is easy to make and Arlo loves it on its own and with yogurt.* 99
> **Cally, mum to Arlo, 6 months**

Blueberry delight (6 months+)

This simple pudding is good for introducing babies to blueberries, which are often described as a 'superfood' because of the host of antioxidants they contain. It's thicker than a fruit purée or yogurt, so easier for babies to manage themselves.

150g blueberries (fresh or frozen)
125ml water
20g oats
1 heaped tbsp cream cheese

Preparation time: 10 minutes.
Equipment: 1 saucepan.
Storage: Fridge for 1–2 days or freeze.
Servings: 6 baby portions.

- Put the blueberries, water and oats in the pan.
- Bring to the boil and simmer for 2–3 minutes until thickened, stirring occasionally.
- Take off the heat and stir in the cream cheese, then divide into portions.

Tips

- This can be eaten warm but it's nice if you put it in the fridge, where it will set slightly.

Peachy pudding (6 months+)

A ripe peach makes a lovely pudding on its own or mashed with a little yogurt. If you have peaches that aren't so good for eating raw or if your baby doesn't like them that way, here is an alternative. Or make this when peaches are at their best so that your baby can enjoy the taste of summer for a little longer.

50g white rice (e.g. basmati)
2 peaches
1 medium banana
4 dried apricots
150ml milk

Preparation time: 20 minutes.
Equipment: 1 saucepan.
Storage: Fridge for 1–2 days or freeze.
Servings: 8 baby portions.

- Place the rice in the pan with 150ml of water. Bring to the boil and simmer until the water has been absorbed.
- Meanwhile, peel the skin off the peaches using a small knife and chop the flesh into small chunks.
- Chop the dried apricots and peel and slice the banana.
- When the rice is ready, add the fruit and milk and bring the mixture back to the boil. Simmer for 5–8 minutes until the fruit is soft.
- Remove from the heat and purée to suit your baby.
- The mixture will thicken as it cools – you can add extra milk to make the pudding a suitable consistency.

Tips

- Add some extra flavour by adding a pinch of cinnamon or half a teaspoon of vanilla essence when you're cooking, or by sprinkling a little cinnamon on top when you give it to your baby.

> 66 *This is delicious and went down very well with Ailsa. I think it will become a firm favourite as it smells divine and I can alter the consistency as she gets better at chewing.* 99
> **Emma, mum to Rory, 3 years, and Ailsa, 6 months**

Raw fruit

Bananas are just about the easiest food to prepare for a baby. There's no need for cooking as they're naturally soft and sweet so you can just mash half a banana in a bowl using a fork or give it as a finger food. Half a banana can be given peeled, but this can prove tricky to handle at first, as it easily slips out of a baby's grasp or gets mushed as it's squeezed in a tight fist. Try leaving the peel on at one end and cutting around it so that your baby has some peel to hold onto like a handle. Or, if she's happy, you can just peel it and leave her to get on with it and learn how to handle it.

Other fruits that can be given raw include ripe pear, peach, plum and melon. Stone fruit can either be cut in half and the stone removed before you give it to your baby or you can keep a close eye and remove it when your baby gets near to it. Small fruits such as grapes and blueberries should be cut in half or squished to avoid choking. Don't give raw apple at this stage, as research with mums using BLW found pieces of apple to be the most common cause of choking.

If you're giving your baby fruit with the peel left on, make sure you give it a good wash. Otherwise bacteria that cause food poisoning, which may be present on the outside, can be transferred to the edible part of the fruit or ingested directly.

Meal plan for a 6-month-old baby

You don't need to follow a meal plan, especially at this age when your baby is just getting used to having a variety of different foods (though do try to make sure that you include some protein and iron-rich foods, such as eggs, lentils, fish and chicken). However, some parents may find the table below useful, even if just to get an idea of what your baby can eat at this stage. This plan is for a baby who has been eating for a couple of weeks and has progressed to having three meals a day and the odd snack some days too.

Day	Breakfast	Snack	Lunch	Snack	Dinner
1	Milk feed Apple purée and baby rice	Milk feed	Roasted butternut squash and red pepper purée (p30) Half a banana (whole or mashed)	Milk feed	Haddock and sweet potato (p46) Milk feed
2	Milk feed Porridge or porridge fingers (p26) and slices of pear	Milk feed Rice cake	Scrambled eggs (p45) with carrot and parsnip purée or sticks (p35)	Milk feed	Spinach, pea and potato purée (p33) and/ or steamed or boiled vegetable sticks (p35) Apple and mango purée (p51) Milk feed

Continued over page

Weaning Made Easy Recipes

Continued from overleaf

Day	Breakfast	Snack	Lunch	Snack	Dinner
3	Milk feed Mashed banana and yogurt	Milk feed	Chicken and vegetable purée (p47) or fingers (p48)	Milk feed	Tagliatelle with green sauce (p39) Half a pear or pear and sultana purée (p52) Milk feed
4	Milk feed Weetabix and banana	Milk feed	Puréed or pieces of beef, potato and carrot (from Sunday roast) Peachy pudding (p55)	Milk feed Red pepper and polenta soldiers (p40)	Yellow split pea dhal (p54) and broccoli florets or purée Fruit Milk feed
5	Milk feed Porridge or porridge fingers (p26)	Milk feed	Leftover potato and carrot Banana and blueberry purée (p52) or other fruit	Milk feed	Chicken and vegetable purée (p47) or fingers (p48) Milk feed

Babies should be given water with each of the meals, even if they drink very little.

Dos, don'ts and FAQs for your 4 to 6-month-old

Do

- Relax and take things slowly.
- Gradually start to introduce solids when your baby shows signs of being ready.
- Start weaning if your baby is 6 months old even if she's not showing obvious signs of being ready.
- Give your baby plenty of savoury foods, especially vegetables, even if she prefers fruit.
- Give finger foods from 6 months old whether you're starting with purées or BLW.
- Stay with your baby while she eats to make sure she's ok and to make mealtimes more enjoyable. Whenever possible, eat the same or similar foods.
- Offer water to drink at every meal.

Don't

- Give your baby anything to eat other than breast or formula milk before she is 4 months old.
- Try to get your baby to finish her meal. Now is the time for experimenting and learning about different foods in a relaxed and fun way.
- Give your baby the same food every day. Swapping around meals encourages more adventurous eating.
- Give meat, eggs, dairy or wheat until your baby is 6 months old.
- Let your baby have too much milk once she's 6 months old, or she'll be too full to eat solids.

FAQs

Q: My daughter's eaten really well since she was 5 months old but doesn't seem to know when to stop. What should I do?

A: Some babies love eating, but it takes their digestive system a little while to adjust so it's important to start slowly. Offer only a few spoonfuls of purée or pieces of vegetable for the first few days, then after that babies should be able to eat as much as they want and stop naturally when they've had enough. If you're spoon-feeding, look out for any signs that she's had enough – obvious ones such as turning her head away or subtle signs such as not opening her mouth so keenly. You can also give more of her meal as finger food, as this will make her eat more slowly and she'll recognise more easily when she's had enough.

Prepare what you think is a reasonable amount of food and if your baby finishes it, don't look worried or apologetic that there's no more. Instead, wipe her face and hands in a playful way and move on to doing other interesting things together.

Q: If I don't give my son nuts or other foods that could cause allergies for a while, will he be less likely to have an allergic reaction?

A: There is no evidence that waiting until babies are older before giving them foods such as nuts, eggs, wheat or dairy is beneficial. These foods can be given from 6 months and research suggests that waiting until your baby is older may even increase the risk of an allergy developing. It can also mean babies miss out on important nutrients.

To reduce the risk of problems, give only a small amount of these foods to start with. Give them one at a time and look out for any signs of an allergic reaction such as breathing problems, skin irritation or an upset stomach. If you have a family history of allergies (including asthma, eczema and hay fever) be particularly careful about introducing peanuts and talk to your GP or health visitor before giving your baby peanuts or foods containing peanuts for the first time.

Q: My daughter's just not interested in eating. What should I do?

A: If your baby is under 6 months then it's best just to wait. Look out for signs that she's ready to start (p2) and try again when it seems to be the right time for her. Don't worry about what other babies the same age are doing.

If your baby is 6 months old, she needs the nutrients that solids provide so try to give her plenty of opportunities to taste different foods, without pestering her to eat them. You can also give her a clean feeding spoon to play with and chew on, so that she can get used to it. Also, make sure she's not having too much milk as this could affect her appetite and interest in solids (p12). Offer food when she's not starving but not full, and also when she is well rested and in a cheerful mood. If she doesn't seem happy in a high chair or bumbo seat with a bib on, try feeding her on your lap for now. If you've been trying purées, maybe give her some finger foods or a little of your own food so that she feels like she's joining in. Or if you've been offering finger foods, maybe try helping her along with a spoon too, for the time being.

Q: Should I buy organic food for my baby?

A: There isn't really any evidence that this is beneficial. Organic foods are produced using fewer pesticides, which would seem preferable, but regulations are in place to ensure that pesticide residues are within safe limits on all foods. Also, organic food may not be pesticide free, as some pesticides are permitted and contamination can occur from neighbouring farms. So going organic won't remove all sources of exposure, although it will reduce them. It is much more important that babies eat well than that they eat organic. The benefits of eating plenty of fruit and vegetables are well established so it's more important to focus your attention here than on providing organic food, for which no such benefits have been shown. If you want to buy some organic food, go for fruits and vegetables that are going to be eaten raw, as processing, including cooking, reduces pesticide levels anyway.

Q: Can I give my baby finger food now?

A: If your baby is 6 months old, then yes, do start to offer some finger foods. There's no harm in trying if your baby is 5 months old, but from about 6 months babies start getting better at sitting up and they naturally put things in their mouths, so they are developmentally more ready. Providing finger foods, either alongside purées or instead of purées, may also help improve your baby's hand–eye co-ordination, as she tries to get bits of food to her mouth, and her pincer grip, as she tries to grasp peas or other small pieces of food.

Sometimes parents are reluctant to offer finger foods because of a fear of choking. However, many are pleasantly surprised at how well their baby copes and how much she enjoys it. Of course, it's important to choose suitable foods – 6-month-olds have either no teeth or not enough to chew properly. Therefore pieces of food should be soft enough to either dissolve or be mushed with gums (p25). If your baby has some finger foods from early on in the weaning process rather than just having purées, it is less likely that you'll have problems when you start moving on to lumpier food, which can sometimes be an issue (p106). Having the opportunity to handle foods can also help babies familiarise themselves with them, and this can help reduce fussy eating.

3 Feeding your 7- to 9-month-old

Between 7 and 9 months, most babies really get into the swing of eating solids. Seven-month-old babies need three meals a day as well as three or four breastfeeds or 500–600ml of formula. Most will also have two small snacks a day. Meals should be well balanced and most should contain carbohydrates (e.g. rice, potato, pasta), protein (e.g. meat, fish, lentils, milk) and some fruit or vegetables. An example would be porridge with milk and dried fruit, or pasta with a lentil and vegetable sauce. Of course, your baby might not eat every element of the balanced meal you provide, but it's good for her to get used to the idea that this is normal. Snacks might be a couple of mini rice cakes or half a banana. The amount of food a baby eats at this stage is relatively small, so it's important that every bite counts. This means snacks should generally be the same healthy foods you're giving at mealtimes.

It's a good idea to establish a regular pattern of meals and snacks at about the same time every day. Your baby will then be more hungry and ready to eat when she's given food. Babies become much more able to feed themselves at this stage and increasingly independent, so it's important to encourage this by giving them plenty of finger foods. They should also be having lumpier meals now, rather than the completely smooth purées they may have started with. To achieve this, you can still use a hand-held blender, but do just a few pulses rather than blending fully. Alternatively, you can mash meals such as pasta or shepherd's pie with a fork, or, if your baby is able to cope with larger lumps, you could chop them roughly with a knife. Some meals, such as omelette and wraps, but also pasta dishes, can be eaten with hands if your baby enjoys them that way. Some take to lumps more easily than others, but it's important that all babies are moving either gradually or more quickly away from purées and on to more textured foods (p106).

Foods to give your baby

Each day, try to give your baby:

- two to three servings of starchy foods (e.g. baby rice, porridge, potato) – these should make up roughly one-third of each meal
- one serving of meat, fish, pulses (e.g. lentils) or well-cooked egg
- two to three servings of fruit and vegetables
- 500–600ml of formula or about three or four breastfeeds.

Variety is also crucial at this stage, so take advantage of the fact that your baby's likes and dislikes won't be too firmly established yet. As the amount of food she eats increases, introduce a range of foods and different types of fish, egg dishes and fruits and vegetables, including beans and lentils. These should be given as finger foods as well as purées. In fact, if you can, do try to make at least some part of every meal a finger food. For example, fish and tomato pie (p84) could be eaten with a spoon but be followed by slices of melon. As your baby has more finger foods, you'll notice her ever-growing skills and ability to feed herself.

Breakfasts

Now that your baby is having breakfast every day, you might be looking for ideas to make it a bit more exciting. It's easy to end up with porridge or plain Weetabix every morning – while these are healthy choices, it's good to introduce some variety, either by adding fruit or nuts to plain cereals, or by having something completely different some days, such as pancakes.

Foods to mix with porridge, Weetabix or other breakfast cereals

- ½ a mashed banana
- 3 chopped dried apricots and 2 tsp ground almonds
- 2 tsp sultanas and ½ a grated apple

- 3 sliced strawberries
- 2 tsp raisins and 2 tsp chopped walnuts
- ½ a diced peach, 1 tbsp natural yogurt and a sprinkle of cinnamon

Fruit and nut porridge

The apricots and almonds in this creamy porridge provide extra iron at a time when babies are particularly vulnerable to anaemia.

1 medium eating apple
5 dried apricots
100ml water
40g porridge oats
1 tbsp ground almonds
250ml milk or dairy-free formula

Preparation time: 20 minutes.
Equipment: 1 saucepan and 1 hand-held blender (optional).
Storage: Fridge for 1–2 days or freeze. Defrost in the fridge or a microwave and add a little extra milk if needed when reheating.
Servings: 3–4 baby portions.

- Peel and core the apple then chop it into 1cm chunks.
- Chop the dried apricots and place them in the pan with the apple and water.
- Bring to the boil and simmer with the lid on for 5 minutes until soft.
- Add the oats, ground almonds and milk, then bring back to the boil and simmer for a few minutes until thick and creamy.
- The porridge can be served as it is or you can mash it slightly with a fork or potato masher, or use a blender to make a smooth purée.

Tips

- If you are just starting to introduce your baby to slightly lumpier meals you can purée the fruit before adding the other ingredients.
- The apricots can be swapped for other dried fruit, such as raisins, sultanas or prunes.
- In place of ground almonds, you could use other ground nuts, such as hazelnuts, Brazil nuts or walnuts. However, you will probably have to chop

these or grind them in a food processor, as they are not usually sold already ground.
- To make a nut-free version simply leave out the nuts and use extra dried fruit instead.

Eggy bread soldiers

Soldiers of eggy bread make great finger food. They take only minutes to cook and can be eaten for breakfast, lunch or tea.

1 egg
1 tbsp milk
1 slice bread (white, granary or wholemeal)
½ tsp butter or margarine for cooking

Preparation time: 5 minutes.
Equipment: 1 small frying pan and 1 bowl.
Storage: Best eaten straight away, but can be kept in the fridge for 24 hours and reheated.
Servings: 1–2 baby portions.

- Crack the egg into the bowl, add the milk and beat with a fork.
- Put the bread in the bowl and push it down gently to soak up the egg. Turn the bread over and push it down again.
- Heat a little butter or margarine in the frying pan, then place the eggy bread in it. If there's any of the egg and milk left in the bowl, pour it on the bread.
- Cook for 1–2 minutes until starting to brown, then flip over and cook the other side.
- Cut the bread into slices, either in the pan with a spatula or after it's cooked.

Tips

- For a tasty breakfast, add a pinch of cinnamon to the egg when you're beating it and serve with puréed apple or fresh banana or strawberries.
- For lunch or tea serve with sliced tomatoes, carrot sticks or roast vegetables.

66 *Emily has a cows' milk intolerance so I made these with olive oil and formula instead of butter and milk. I also blended in some cherry tomatoes with the egg. It worked really well.* 99
Katherine, mum to Emily, 8 months

Breakfast ideas

- Fruit purée mixed with baby rice
- Porridge made with oats and milk
- Porridge fingers (p26)
- Baby breakfasts containing cereals and fruit with added iron and vitamins
- Instant hot oat cereal (e.g. Ready Brek)
- Weetabix or similar cereals
- Pancakes (pp27, 28 and p111)
- Eggy bread
- Scrambled eggs (p45) and toast fingers

Lunches and dinners

Lunch and dinner foods are pretty much the same for babies at this age. Babies can have hot meals such as shepherd's pie, chicken stew or fish at both lunchtime and in the evening – this is what you'll see in many traditional weaning plans. However, most adults don't eat like this and there's no need for babies to. If you can eat with your baby at lunchtime, then it's lovely to share soup, an omelette or toast and one of the dips or pâtés here. Then you could make a hot meal in the evening. Some parents find that eating together in the evening doesn't work because they need to eat at different times. However, if you choose to make a baby-friendly meal for yourself in the evening, your baby can always have it for lunch the next day. There is a mixture of baby recipes and family recipes in this section, and don't forget that leftover vegetables and other foods can often be turned into a tasty baby meal, which saves you time and helps your baby get used to the foods you eat.

Salmon pâté

This makes a lovely quick weekend lunch, spread on wholemeal toast with some sliced tomato.

1 salmon fillet or steak
75g fromage frais or yogurt
½ medium ripe avocado
1 tsp lemon juice

Preparation time: 10 minutes.
Equipment: 2 bowls.
Storage: Fridge for 24 hours.
Servings: 2 adults and 1 baby.

- Place the salmon in a microwave-safe bowl and drizzle half of the lemon juice on top.
- Cover the bowl with cling film, pierce with a fork and microwave for about 1½ minutes until cooked.
- Using a fork, flake the fish into the clean bowl, leaving behind any skin and bones.
- Cut the avocado in half, scoop out the flesh and mash it, along with the fromage frais and salmon. Add lemon juice and black pepper to taste.

Tips

- Adults, and some babies, might like to have this with some finely chopped spring onion.
- This works just as well with trout instead of salmon, and yogurt or cream cheese in place of fromage frais.

> 66 *Everyone liked this. Really great as a change from the endless cheese sandwiches Elizabeth has for lunch usually.* 99
> **Emma, mum to Elizabeth, 14 months**

Butter bean and parsley pâté

A fresh tasting pâté with lemon and parsley, which tastes great on wholemeal toast.

1 tsp olive oil
2 shallots
1 garlic clove, crushed
1 × 400g tin butter beans
2 tsp lemon juice
3 tbsp natural yogurt (or ½ an avocado for a dairy-free version)
2 tbsp fresh parsley, chopped

Preparation time: 10–15 minutes.
Equipment: 1 small frying pan and 1 blender jug.
Storage: Fridge for 1–2 days or freeze.
Servings: 2 adults and 1 baby.

- Peel and finely dice the shallots.
- Heat the oil in the frying pan and fry the shallots and crushed garlic for about 5 minutes until soft.
- Drain the butter beans and place in the blender, along with the lemon juice and yogurt. Purée roughly so that the pâté still has a coarse texture.
- Stir in the shallot mixture and chopped parsley.

Butternut squash and sage dip

A lovely creamy dip that's perfect with wholemeal pitta soldiers or potato wedges and strips of roasted red pepper.

1 butternut squash
2 tsp olive oil
2 tbsp cream cheese
8–10 sage leaves
1 tsp lemon juice
pinch of cumin (optional)

Preparation time: 10 minutes plus 20–30 minutes roasting.
Equipment: 1 roasting tin, and 1 food processor or 1 deep-sided bowl and hand-held blender.
Storage: Fridge for 1–2 days or freeze.
Servings: 4 adults or 15–20 baby portions.

- Preheat the oven to 220°C/425°F/gas mark 7.
- Cut the squash in half lengthways. Scoop out the seeds and membrane with a spoon and discard.
- Cut each half of the squash again lengthways so that you have four pieces.
- Brush the pieces with oil and arrange in the roasting tin.
- Roast in the oven for 20–30 minutes until soft.
- When the squash is cool enough to handle, scoop the flesh out of the skin and place in the food processor.
- Finely chop the sage leaves and add to the food processor along with the cumin, if using, cream cheese and lemon juice.
- Purée until smooth.

Soya bean and pea houmous

This makes a tasty alternative to the ever-popular chickpea houmous. It's a good source of protein and iron and is cheap and easy to make.

> 250g frozen soya beans (edamame)
> 150g frozen peas
> 1 garlic clove, crushed
> juice of ½ lemon
> 1 tbsp olive oil
> 1 tbsp natural yogurt

Preparation time: 15 minutes.
Equipment: 1 saucepan.
Storage: Fridge for 2–3 days or freeze.
Servings: 2 pots of houmous, one for the fridge and the other for freezing.

- Bring 100ml of water to the boil in a saucepan then add the beans and peas. Bring back to the boil, and simmer for 3–4 minutes with the lid on.
- Drain the cooking water into a cup or jug and set aside. Fill the pan with cold water to cool the beans and peas, then drain. Pour the cold water away.
- Add the crushed garlic, lemon juice, yogurt and oil, then blend. Add as much of the cooking water as needed to make a good houmous-like texture.

Tips

- Serve with toasted pitta bread and vegetable sticks. It also tastes good with salmon and spring onion rösti (p175).
- To make a dairy-free version simply leave out the yogurt or replace it with some avocado.
- Having this with a high vitamin C pudding such as fresh strawberries or kiwi will boost iron absorption from the dip.

Wraps

These are the simplest type of bread you can possibly make and are delicious served warm with dips or chilli.

> 300g plain flour
> 100ml warm water
> 20ml olive or rapeseed oil

Preparation time: 40 minutes.
Equipment: 1 non-stick frying pan or griddle and 1 mixing bowl.

Storage: Best eaten straight away or freeze, then sprinkle with water and reheat in the oven.
Servings: 8 wraps.

- Put the flour in the mixing bowl and make a well in the centre.
- Add the oil and water and use a fork to bring in the flour from the edges to combine the ingredients.
- Using one hand, bring together the mixture to form a ball.
- Turn the dough out onto a floured work surface and knead for 5 minutes.
- Divide the ball of dough in half, then repeat until you have eight pieces.
- Take one piece of dough in each hand and knead for a minute more to make a smooth ball. (This is quite good for stress relief too!)
- Put the frying pan on the hob and heat until very hot, then turn down to medium. Roll out the first piece of dough until it's as thin as possible and about the size of a small plate.
- Dust off any excess flour and put the wrap in the pan for about 30 seconds, until the edges start to look cooked.
- Flip the wrap over and do the same on the other side.
- While one wrap is cooking you can roll out the next.
- Put the cooked wraps on a plate covered with a damp tea towel to stop them drying out.

Corn flatbreads

These are made in a similar way to wraps but tend to end up smaller, and crispy rather than soft.

300g cornmeal/maize flour
200ml warm water
20ml olive or rapeseed oil
plain flour for dusting

Preparation time: 40 minutes.
Equipment: 1 non-stick frying pan or griddle and 1 mixing bowl.
Storage: Best eaten straight away or freeze, then sprinkle with water and reheat in the oven.
Servings: 8 flatbreads.

- Put the cornmeal in the mixing bowl and make a well in the centre.
- Add the oil and water and use a fork to bring in the flour from the edges to combine the ingredients.

- Using one hand, bring together the mixture to form a ball.
- The dough is fairly delicate and can't really be kneaded like regular bread dough, but try gently kneading it for a few minutes.
- Divide the dough in half, then repeat until you have 8 pieces.
- Take one piece of dough and form it into a ball, then place it on a piece of cling film or greaseproof paper sprinkled with a little plain flour.
- Put another piece of cling film or greaseproof paper on top, then using a rolling pin gently roll out the dough until it is 2–3mm thick.
- Put the frying pan on the hob and heat until very hot, then turn down to medium.
- Gently put the flatbread in the pan for about 30 seconds to 1 minute, until the edges start to look cooked.
- Turn the flatbread over and do the same on the other side.
- While one flatbread is cooking you can roll out the next.
- Put the cooked flatbreads on a plate covered with a damp tea towel to stop them drying out.

Tips

- Cornmeal looks like wheat flour that you would use for making cakes and biscuits, but it is pale yellow. Don't confuse this with polenta, which is also made from corn but appears grittier and more like sand than soft flour. It is also different from cornflour, which is basically just the starch from the corn, and is used for thickening custard or gravy.

Cream of vegetable soup

This is a creamy soup that isn't made with cream. You can make it with just about any vegetables you like. It's a good way of getting vegetables into babies who can be a bit fussy and for getting milk into those who seem to have gone off it.

2 tsp olive or rapeseed oil
1 onion
1 medium carrot
3–4 mushrooms
3 broccoli florets
½ medium courgette
1 bay leaf
1 heaped tbsp plain flour (white, wholemeal or gluten-free)
500ml milk

Preparation time: 30 minutes.
Equipment: 1 saucepan and 1 hand-held blender (optional).
Storage: Fridge for 24 hours or freeze.
Servings: 2 adults and 1 baby or 10 baby portions.

- Peel and dice the onion.
- Heat the oil in the pan, then stir in the onion, put a lid on the pan and leave to sweat for 2–3 minutes. Don't let the onion brown.
- Peel the carrot, then chop all the vegetables into thin slices or cubes.
- Add the vegetables to the pan along with the bay leaf. Stir, then leave to cook on a low heat with the lid on for about 15 minutes until all the vegetables are tender.
- Add the flour and stir it in thoroughly.
- Add about half the milk and stir well.
- Mix in the remaining milk and bring to the boil, still stirring. Continue to cook for a few minutes until thickened.
- Remove the bay leaf and serve the soup as it is or use a blender to make it smooth.

Tips

- If you want to make this thicker simply add less milk.
- You can also add peas, cauliflower, celery, parsnips, cabbage or other vegetables.
- You can add potato to make it into a more substantial meal on its own, or have it with leftover pasta.

Baked courgette fingers

These are surprisingly sweet and tasty and likely to be enjoyed by adults as well as babies.

1 large or 2 small courgettes
1 tbsp olive oil (plus extra for greasing)
50g oats
1 tbsp fresh parsley, finely chopped
50g Cheddar cheese, grated
1 egg

Preparation time: 30 minutes plus 10–15 minutes cooking.
Equipment: 1 frying pan and 1 baking tray.

Storage: Fridge for 1–2 days or freeze. Reheat in the oven or under the grill.
Servings: 12–14 fingers – babies might eat 1 or 2.

- Preheat the oven to 200°C/400°F/gas mark 6.
- Cut the ends off the courgettes and finely dice. Don't remove the skin or you'll lose lots of nutrients.
- Heat the oil in a frying pan and fry the courgette for about 10 minutes until soft and slightly browned.
- Brush the baking tray with oil and place in the oven.
- Leave the courgette to cool for a few minutes, then mix in the oats, parsley and cheese.
- Mix the egg with the rest of the ingredients, then take walnut-sized pieces, form them into sausage shapes and place them on the baking tray.
- Bake for 10–15 minutes until browned on the outside. Turn over halfway through.

Tips

- These go well with avocado and yogurt dip (p43).

> 66 *These are delicious and both my children enjoyed them.* 99
> **Zuza, mum to Max, 5 years, and Ruby, 7 months**

Parsnip fritters

These are fairly soft but they don't fall apart too easily, so they're great for babies just getting to grips with finger foods.

5 large parsnips
100g plain flour
2 tsp baking powder
150ml milk
1 egg
1–2 tbsp rapeseed oil

Preparation time: 40 minutes.
Equipment: 1 frying pan and 1 mixing bowl.
Storage: Fridge for 1–2 days or freeze in a freezer bag or airtight container, separated by sheets of greaseproof paper or baking parchment. Reheat under the grill.
Servings: 18 fritters – babies might eat 1 or 2.

- Peel the parsnips, cut the ends off, and cut into chunks.
- Steam the parsnips or boil with a little water for 10–15 minutes until soft but not mushy.
- Turn the cooked parsnips out onto a chopping board and chop the whole pile roughly into small pieces.
- Put the flour and baking powder into a bowl and make a well in the centre.
- Crack the egg into the centre and add the milk, then beat with a fork or wire whisk.
- Add the cooked parsnip to the mixture and stir.
- Heat a little oil in a frying pan until sizzling, then place mounds of the mixture into the pan (about a tablespoon of mixture for each).
- When the edges look cooked and bubbles start to appear, turn over with a spatula or fish slice and cook the other side. Each side should take 2–3 minutes.

Tips

- You can substitute courgette or aubergine for parsnips, or use a mixture of vegetables.

Falafel

This basic recipe is easy to adjust by using different beans, or you can leave out the flour or sesame seeds or add an egg, depending on your baby's needs.

½ small onion
1 × 400g tin chickpeas
2 tsp sesame seeds or tahini
1 garlic clove
1 tsp ground cumin
1 tsp ground coriander
2 tbsp plain flour
2 tbsp chopped parsley
1 tbsp vegetable oil

Preparation time: 20 minutes.
Equipment: 1 frying pan and 1 food processor or a deep-sided bowl and hand-held blender.
Storage: Fridge for 1–2 days or freeze. Reheat in the oven or under the grill.
Servings: 2 adults and 1 baby – 10 –12 walnut-sized falafel.

- Peel and finely dice the onion and sauté in a little oil for 3–4 minutes.
- Drain the chickpeas and put all the ingredients, apart from the oil but including the cooked onion, into a food processor or mixing bowl and purée until smooth.
- Shape the mixture into 10–12 walnut-sized balls. These can be flattened slightly or left as they are.
- Heat the oil in the frying pan and fry the falafel for about 5 minutes.

Tips

- These can be eaten with salad and yogurt dressing (see below) in a wrap.

Yogurt dressing

This goes very nicely with falafel and lots of other finger foods.

100ml plain yogurt
1 tsp lemon juice
pinch of cumin

Preparation time: Less than 5 minutes.
Equipment: 1 bowl or jug.
Storage: Fridge for 1–2 days.
Servings: 2 adults and 1 baby.

- Simply mix all the ingredients together.

Baked aubergine and lentils

This rich, tomato-flavoured dhal with aubergines goes well with rice, pasta, baked potatoes or mash.

1 tbsp olive oil
1 onion
1 medium aubergine
2 cloves garlic, crushed
¼ tsp ground cinnamon
½ tsp ground cumin
½ tsp ground coriander
125g red lentils
2 tbsp tomato purée
1 low salt stock cube made up with 500ml boiling water

Preparation time: 20 minutes plus 30 minutes cooking.
Equipment: 1 ovenproof saucepan or casserole dish with lid.
Storage: Fridge for 1–2 days or freeze.
Servings: 2 adults and 2 babies.

- Preheat the oven to 180°C/350°F/gas mark 4.
- Dice the onion and aubergine into 1cm cubes. Start by slicing the aubergine lengthways, then cutting the slices into sticks and then cut these into cubes.
- Heat the oil in the pan, then fry the onion and aubergine, with the crushed garlic, for about 5 minutes until soft.
- Add the spices and stir for a minute.
- Add the tomato purée and lentils followed by the stock. Bring to the boil, then cover and place in the oven for 30 minutes. If you leave it longer it will be fine.

Tips

- This tastes good with a squeeze of lemon juice on top or with yogurt dressing (p76).
- If your baby doesn't usually like aubergine or other foods with a slightly slimy texture, such as avocado, then mash or blend the dhal slightly.

    66 *This was easy to make. The flavours were subtle but tasty, and we all enjoyed it.* 99
    Laura, mum to Sofia, 3 years, and Emilia, 9 months

Vegetarian cottage pie with sweet potato mash

A simple midweek supper for adults and children, and any leftovers freeze well for your baby to enjoy another day.

2 large sweet potatoes
2 tsp olive oil
1 small onion
1 medium carrot
3 mushrooms
1 × 400g tin green lentils
½ × 400g tin chopped tomatoes
1 tbsp tomato purée

> 1 bay leaf
> 1 tbsp fresh thyme, chopped, or 1 tsp dried thyme
> 10g butter or margarine
> 25g Cheddar cheese, grated

Preparation time: 30 minutes plus 20 minutes cooking.
Equipment: 1 saucepan, 1 deep-sided frying pan with lid and 1 ovenproof dish.
Storage: Fridge for 1–2 days or freeze.
Servings: 2 adults and 2 babies or 12–14 baby portions.

- Peel the sweet potatoes and cut them into small chunks. Place them in the saucepan, cover with water, bring to the boil and simmer for about 15 minutes until soft.
- Meanwhile, peel and chop the onion and carrot and slice the mushrooms.
- Preheat the oven to 190°C/375°F/gas mark 5.
- Heat the oil in the frying pan and sauté the onion for 2–3 minutes, then add the carrot and mushroom and cook for another 5 minutes.
- Add the drained lentils, chopped tomatoes, tomato purée, bay leaf and thyme. Bring to the boil, then put the lid on and simmer for 10 minutes until everything is cooked through. Taste a piece of carrot to check it's soft.
- Drain the sweet potatoes and mash them with the butter or margarine.
- Pour the lentil mixture into the ovenproof dish and spoon the mashed potato over the top. Smooth it roughly with a fork, then cover with grated cheese.
- Bake for 20 minutes until cooked through and browned on top. You might want to place the dish under the grill for a few minutes to finish it off.

Tips

- Babies need more fat in their diets than adults so you might want to grate more cheese on one end of the dish than the other.
- For a dairy-free version, leave out the cheese and dot the top with a little extra margarine before baking.
- This is good with some peas on the side. Adults might want to add some Worcestershire sauce or brown sauce.

Lentil and vegetable cobbler

During the Second World War, the Ministry of Food promoted cobblers as a good alternative to pies, as they contain less fat and butter was rationed. This makes them a healthier choice too, but still a hearty dinner for cold days. This one has the added advantage of containing about 10 portions of vegetables in total!

2 tsp olive oil
1 garlic clove, crushed
1 small onion
1 medium courgette
2 medium carrots
50g dried red lentils
1 × 400g tin chopped tomatoes
1 tsp dried mixed herbs
1 bay leaf
½ low salt stock cube made up with 250ml boiling water
1 tbsp cornflour

For the scone topping:
100g self-raising flour (or gluten-free flour)
25g butter or margarine
40g Cheddar cheese, grated
1 egg
50–75ml milk

Preparation time: 45 minutes plus 15 minutes cooking.
Equipment: 1 deep-sided frying pan and 1 casserole dish.
Storage: Best eaten straight away or freeze the scone and filling separately.
Servings: 2 adults and 1–2 babies.

- Peel and dice the onion and carrots and dice the courgette into 1cm cubes.
- Heat the oil in the frying pan and sauté the onion and crushed garlic for 2–3 minutes.
- Add the carrot and courgette and continue cooking for a few minutes longer.
- Add the tinned tomato, lentils, herbs and stock and bring to the boil.
- Mix the cornflour with two tablespoons of cold water and stir into the mixture.
- Simmer the vegetables and lentils for about 20 minutes.
- Meanwhile, prepare the scone topping and preheat the oven to 200°C/400°F/gas mark 6.
- Rub the butter or margarine into the flour until it resembles fine breadcrumbs.

- Add the egg and grated cheese to the mixture and enough milk to form a dough.
- Turn the dough out onto a floured surface and roll with a floured rolling pin to about 1cm thickness. Using a biscuit cutter or, if you don't have one, a cup, cut out circles of dough. Re-roll the off-cuts and repeat until the dough is all used up. You will be able to make about eight scones.
- When the filling is ready, pour it into the casserole dish and place the scones on top in a ring around the edge. Any leftover scones can go in the middle.
- Brush the tops of the scones with a little milk and place the dish in the oven for 15 minutes, until the scones are golden brown on top.

Tips

- This is a great meal for babies who can feed themselves the scone topping while you help them along with a spoon to eat the filling.
- Instead of lentils you can use a tin of chickpeas or beans, such as cannellini or butter beans.
- Instead of rolling out the dough and making scones, you can just place large spoonfuls of the dough mixture on top of the lentil mixture.
- To make an egg-free version just leave out the egg and use extra milk instead.

Macaroni cheese

This has a very mild flavour and is ideal for babies who would usually rather eat their pasta plain.

> 150g macaroni (or other pasta)
> 300ml milk
> 20g plain flour
> 1 tbsp butter or margarine
> 1 bay leaf
> ½ tsp Dijon mustard (optional)
> pinch of nutmeg (optional)
> 50g frozen peas
> 75g mature Cheddar cheese

Preparation time: 20 minutes plus 10–15 minutes in the oven if you want to brown the top.
Equipment: 2 saucepans and 1 ovenproof dish.

Storage: Fridge for 1–2 days or freeze.
Servings: 2 adults and 1 baby or 12–14 baby portions.

- Cook the pasta according to the instructions on the packet.
- To make the sauce, put the milk, flour, butter or margarine and bay leaf into another saucepan. Bring to the boil, stirring all the time, then simmer for a couple of minutes.
- Turn the heat off under the sauce. Grate about half the cheese into the pan, add the mustard and nutmeg, if using, and stir.
- When the pasta is almost ready, add the peas to the pan of pasta and bring back to the boil.
- Drain the pasta and peas and combine with the cheese sauce, then transfer the mixture to the ovenproof dish.
- Grate the remaining cheese over the top and place in the oven for 10–15 minutes, until heated through and browned on top. Alternatively, just mix in the remaining cheese, mash or purée for your baby and divide into portions for freezing.

Tips

- For babies who want to feed themselves, use pasta bows instead of macaroni as these are easier to grip.
- You can add other vegetables such as cauliflower, broccoli, carrot or fried peppers and mushrooms.

Cheese and chive oven omelette

This is like a quiche without the pastry, and much healthier as pastry is high in fat and contains few useful nutrients. You can put any filling you like in it and it's easier to make than a traditional omelette as it looks after itself in the oven while you prepare the rest of the meal.

4 eggs
100ml milk
20g Cheddar cheese
1 tbsp chopped chives
butter or margarine for greasing

Preparation time: 5 minutes plus 25 minutes cooking.
Equipment: 1 flan dish or other ovenproof dish and 1 large measuring jug.
Storage: Best eaten straight away.
Servings: 2 adults and 1 baby.

- Preheat the oven to 180°C/350°F/gas mark 4.
- Grease the ovenproof dish.
- Pour the milk into a measuring jug.
- Grate the cheese and snip the chives into the milk.
- Crack the eggs into the jug and beat with a fork or electric whisk until the surface is covered in bubbles.
- Pour the mixture into the dish and place in the oven for about 25 minutes, until nicely risen and golden brown.

Tips

- Serve with some salad and bread.
- Instead of Cheddar and chives, try cooked broccoli and salmon, tuna and sweetcorn, boiled potatoes or roasted peppers.

Tomato and mushroom tortilla

This is very simple to make and easy for babies to pick up. You can make it with whatever veg you have to hand.

1 tsp vegetable oil
2 mushrooms
1 medium tomato
3 eggs

Preparation time: 10 minutes.
Equipment: 1 frying pan.
Storage: Eat straight away or fridge for 24 hours.
Servings: 1 adult and 1 baby.

- Cut the mushrooms in half, then slice thinly.
- Cut the tomato into small pieces.
- Heat the oil in the pan and fry the mushroom for 2 minutes, then add the tomato and fry for another 1–2 minutes.
- Meanwhile beat the eggs in a jug or mug.
- Make sure the vegetables are spread fairly evenly over the bottom of the pan, then add the eggs, tilting the pan to spread them out.
- After a few minutes, when the bottom of the tortilla is cooked, put the pan under the grill to cook the top.

Tips

- Serve with bread and vegetable sticks for lunch, or inside pitta, or have it for dinner with potatoes and cooked vegetables.
- Other good combinations are potato and onion, red pepper and courgette, and spring onion and peas.

Cod with sweet peppers

A simple fish dish with a tasty pepper and tomato sauce.

2 tsp olive oil
1 small onion
½ red pepper
½ yellow pepper
½ × 400g tin chopped tomatoes
1 tbsp tomato purée
1 tbsp fresh thyme, chopped, or 1 tsp dried thyme
½ tsp Worcestershire sauce
2 cod fillets or other firm white fish

Preparation time: 25 minutes.
Equipment: 1 deep-sided frying pan with lid.
Storage: Fridge for 1–2 days or freeze.
Servings: 2 adults and 1 baby.

- Chop the onion and peppers into 1cm cubes. Or, if your baby's going to eat with her hands, cut the pepper into thin strips.
- Heat the oil in the pan and sauté the onion and peppers for 5 minutes.
- Add the tomatoes, tomato purée, Worcestershire sauce and thyme, then bring to the boil and simmer for 5 minutes with the lid on.
- Add the fish fillets to the pan, bring it back to a gentle simmer and cook for about 5 minutes, until the fish is cooked through.

Tips

- Serve with rice or new potatoes and broccoli.
- Mash your baby's portion if she would prefer it this way.

Grilled fish with watercress sauce

Grilling salmon or trout is just about the easiest way of preparing it and this sauce provides extra antioxidants, including beta-carotene and selenium. The watercress flavour isn't that strong when mixed with cream cheese.

2 salmon steaks or fillets, or trout fillets
¼ lemon
½ bag of mixed watercress, spinach and rocket (about 40g)
3 tbsp cream cheese

Preparation time: 10–15 minutes.
Equipment: 1 baking tray and 1 blender jug.
Storage: Fridge for 1–2 days or freeze.
Servings: 2 adults and 1 baby.

- Preheat the grill to medium/high.
- Cover the baking tray with foil to make cleaning easier. Place the salmon in the centre, squeeze the lemon juice on top, and grill for about 5 minutes on each side. If the salmon has skin on, grill it with the skin at the top first and add the lemon juice when you turn it over.
- Put the green leaves and cream cheese in the beaker of your food processor and blend for a couple of minutes until smooth.
- Remove the skin from your baby's fish, then place a spoonful of sauce beside each portion. Babies can use it as a dip or have it mixed up together.

Tips

- This tastes great with new potatoes, carrots and broccoli.
- If you can't find bags of mixed leaves, just use watercress. As an alternative to cream cheese, you can use mascarpone or crème fraîche.
- As an alternative to grilling, you can cook salmon in the microwave (p132).

Fish and tomato pie

Traditional fish pies made with white sauce can taste stodgy, but this healthier version is extremely tasty and easy to make.

3–4 medium potatoes
1–2 tsp olive oil
1 small onion
1 garlic clove, crushed

1 × 400g tin chopped tomatoes
1 tbsp tomato purée
1 bay leaf
1 tsp dried mixed herbs
¼ tsp sugar
2 pieces of fish or 250g mixed fish (e.g. salmon and coley)
10g butter or margarine
75ml milk

Preparation time: 30 minutes plus 25 minutes cooking.
Equipment: 2 saucepans and 1 ovenproof dish.
Storage: Fridge for 1–2 days or freeze.
Servings: 2 adults and 1 baby.

- Peel and chop the potatoes and place them in a saucepan. Cover with water, bring to the boil and simmer for 10–15 minutes until soft.
- Preheat the oven to 220°C/425°F/gas mark 7
- Meanwhile, dice the onion and sauté with the oil and garlic for 2–3 minutes until soft.
- Add the tinned tomatoes, purée, bay leaf, herbs and sugar and bring to the boil, then simmer for 5 minutes.
- While the sauce is cooking, cut the fish into bite-sized chunks. Add them to the pan with the tomato mixture, stir and cook for a few minutes until the fish looks just about done.
- When the potatoes are ready, drain them and mash with the butter or margarine and milk.
- Pour the fish mixture into the ovenproof dish, then spoon the mashed potato on top and smooth over with a fork.
- Bake for 20–30 minutes until the potato is starting to brown and the filling is bubbling.

Tips

- Purée slightly with a blender if necessary.
- You can make this with any fish, but a mixture of oily fish and white fish works well. Instead of salmon and coley, you could use mackerel and haddock or trout and river cobbler. Tinned mackerel is fine, as are frozen fish fillets.
- Serve with vegetables on the side, such as broccoli, carrots or peas.
- If you're making this for the freezer you can bake it as described, to brown the top, or just cook the filling until the fish is properly cooked through, then divide into portions.

66 *We love this! It is now a favourite for both Lyra and us adults. We've never had this combination before but it seems obvious once you have it. I've found myself mentioning it to other mums a lot.* **99**
Sophie, mum to Lyra, 9 months

Mackerel and tomato pasta

Mackerel is quite a meaty fish and its flavour is really complemented here by tomato to make a satisfying sauce. You can use fresh mackerel but it can be fiddly to remove the bones, so tinned is used here to be on the safe side.

1 tbsp rapeseed oil
1 onion
1 garlic clove, crushed
½ red pepper
4 mushrooms
1 × 400g tin chopped tomatoes
2 × 125g tins mackerel in brine or sunflower oil
2 tbsp tomato purée
2 tsp dried mixed herbs
¼ tsp sugar
pasta

Preparation time: 25 minutes.
Equipment: 1 deep-sided frying pan and 1 saucepan.
Storage: Fridge for 24 hours or freeze.
Servings: 2 adults and 1 baby.

- Cook the pasta according to the instructions on the packet.
- Dice the onion and pepper and slice the mushrooms.
- Heat the oil in the pan and sauté the vegetables along with the crushed garlic for 8–10 minutes until soft.
- Add the tomatoes, tomato purée, herbs and sugar. Mix and leave to simmer for 5 minutes.
- Drain the mackerel well to remove the oil or brine, fill the tin with water to rinse and drain again, then add the fish to the pan. Stir and cook for a few minutes more until heated through, then stir through the cooked pasta.

Tips

- Tinned mackerel usually has added salt, whether you buy it in brine, oil or tomato sauce. However, you can remove most of this by draining and rinsing the fish.
- You can use tuna instead for a change, but bear in mind that it doesn't contain the beneficial long-chain omega 3 fatty acids found in oily fish such as mackerel, sardines and pilchards.

Pasta with chicken and broccoli

This pasta dish includes all the food groups and is a simple family meal that babies can eat mashed up or with their fingers.

2 tsp olive oil
2 chicken breasts (about 250g)
1 small onion
4 mushrooms
1 garlic clove, crushed
½ head of broccoli
juice and zest of ½ lemon
1 heaped tsp mixed herbs
2 tbsp cream cheese (optional)
1 tbsp Parmesan or pecorino cheese, grated (optional)
1 heaped tbsp walnuts, finely chopped (optional)
farfalle (pasta bows) or fusilli (twists)

Preparation time: 25 minutes.
Equipment: 1 deep-sided frying pan with lid and 1 saucepan.
Storage: Fridge for 1–2 days or freeze.
Servings: 2 adults and 1 baby or 12 baby portions.

- Cook the pasta according to the instructions on the packet.
- Toast the chopped walnuts in the frying pan for a few minutes, then set aside.
- Cut the chicken into strips.
- Heat one teaspoon of oil in the frying pan and fry the chicken for 4–5 minutes until browned all over. Set aside with the walnuts.
- Meanwhile, dice the onion and slice the mushrooms.
- Cut the broccoli into florets, then cut each floret into quarters lengthways. This way the broccoli will cook quickly but still be easy to pick up.

- Heat the second teaspoon of oil in the frying pan and cook the onion, mushrooms and garlic for 1–2 minutes.
- Add the broccoli and cook for about 5 minutes on a medium low heat.
- Return the chicken and walnuts to the pan and add the herbs, lemon juice and zest, cream cheese (if using) and about 50ml of water (you can use water from the pasta pan).
- Stir and leave for a few minutes until everything is cooked through.
- Stir in the grated cheese, if using, and serve with the cooked pasta.

Tips

- If you are mashing or puréeing your baby's portion a bit, you might want to add a little milk or water.

Mini pork and apple patties

These little patties are perfect for little hands to hold without them falling apart too easily. They're a cross between a burger, a meatball and meatloaf.

200g lean minced pork
1 medium apple
1 slice of bread or about 40g wholemeal breadcrumbs
25g Cheddar cheese
rapeseed oil for greasing

Preparation time: 15 minutes plus 30 minutes cooking.
Equipment: 1 muffin tin, 1 mixing bowl and 1 food processor.
Storage: Fridge for 1–2 days or freeze.
Servings: 12 mini patties or 6–12 baby portions.

- Preheat the oven to 180°C/350°F/gas mark 4.
- Grease the muffin tin.
- Prepare the breadcrumbs using a food processor.
- Peel, core and grate the apple into the mixing bowl.
- Grate the cheese into the bowl and add the breadcrumbs and mince.
- Mix everything together well using a fork.
- Divide the mixture between the 12 holes in the muffin tin and press the mixture down with the back of a spoon.
- Bake for about 30 minutes until browned.

Tips
- Serve with sweet potato wedges and vegetables or with pasta and basic tomato sauce (p38).

Preparing meat as finger food

Your baby can have roast chicken or other meat that you're having and it's fairly easy to prepare it for eating with fingers.

- You can give her meat cut into strips, like the vegetables she's probably already had. An ideal size seems to be about 5cm long. With red meat such as beef it is best to cut across the fibres, then your baby can pull it apart more easily.

- Some parents find chicken legs and chops work well because babies can grasp them. If you do this, remove any skin or visible fat or gristle, which your baby could choke on.

- Some parents prefer to give minced meat such as bolognese, or to cut chicken and meat into tiny pea-sized pieces and put those on the high chair tray. With tender meat, such as lamb shank (p90), you can take off shreds for your baby.

- You can also make finger foods with puréed or ground chicken or meat, such as chicken and vegetables fingers (p48) or mini pork and apple patties (p88).

Chicken and spring vegetable one-pot

This is a complete meal, including meat, potatoes and two veg all cooked together. It's ideal for days when one parent eats with the baby and the other eats later, as it tastes just as good warmed up. It also tastes great the next day with crusty bread to mop up the sauce.

2 tsp olive or rapeseed oil
2 chicken thighs or breasts
3 shallots
1 garlic clove, crushed
2 medium potatoes
1 medium carrot
handful of green beans (about 100g)
1 tbsp plain flour
1 tsp Dijon mustard
1 low salt stock cube made up with 300ml boiling water

> juice of ¼ lemon
> 50ml milk
> 1 tbsp fresh parsley, chopped

Preparation time: 20 minutes plus 30 minutes cooking.
Equipment: 1 large saucepan with lid.
Storage: Fridge for 1–2 days or freeze.
Servings: 2 adults and 1 baby.

- Peel the carrot and potatoes. Slice the carrot into 1cm slices, dice the potatoes into 2cm cubes and cut the beans into 2–3cm pieces.
- Cut the chicken into bite-sized pieces.
- Heat one teaspoon of oil in the pan and fry the chicken for 3–4 minutes until browned all over, then transfer to a bowl or plate and set aside.
- Peel and slice the shallots.
- Add the second teaspoon of oil to the pan and cook the shallots, crushed garlic, potatoes, carrots and beans for 3–4 minutes.
- Sprinkle the flour over the vegetables and add the mustard, then stir until the vegetables are coated and mix in the stock.
- Bring to the boil and simmer for 25–30 minutes with the lid on, stirring occasionally.
- Stir in the milk followed by the lemon juice and parsley and serve.

Lamb shank with tomato and rosemary

This takes a long time to cook but the end result is a tasty family meal with meat that falls off the bone, so even babies without any teeth can enjoy it. Perfect with new potatoes or mash and peas and carrots.

> 1 tbsp olive or rapeseed oil
> 2 tbsp plain flour
> 2 lamb shanks
> 6 shallots
> 2 cloves garlic, crushed
> 100ml red grape juice
> 2 tbsp balsamic vinegar
> 1 × 400g tin chopped tomatoes
> 1 tbsp chopped fresh rosemary
> 1 tbsp cornflour

Preparation time: 25 minutes plus 2½ hours cooking.
Equipment: 1 ovenproof saucepan with lid or casserole dish.
Storage: Fridge for 1–2 days or freeze.
Servings: 2 adults and 1 baby plus extra for the freezer.

- Preheat the oven to 160°C/320°F/gas mark 3.
- Peel and slice the shallots.
- Put the lamb shanks on a plate and sprinkle them with flour, or roll them in the flour.
- Heat the oil in the saucepan and cook the lamb for 4–5 minutes, turning frequently, until browned all over. Remove from the pan and set aside.
- Add the shallots and garlic to the pan and fry for 3–4 minutes until soft.
- Add the grape juice, vinegar, chopped tomatoes and rosemary and stir well.
- Return the lamb to the pan and spoon the sauce over the top. Bring to the boil, then put the lid on and place in the oven for 2½ hours.
- When the lamb is ready, mix the cornflour with a little cold water, then stir into the sauce to thicken it.

Baked Roman gnocchi

Gnocchi are usually made from potato, but in Rome they traditionally use semolina instead. Authentic recipes also include huge amounts of butter and Parmesan cheese but this is a healthier version that is great for lunch with some salad or for dinner with a simple tomato sauce. The gnocchi are creamy inside but crispy enough on the outside for little hands to pick them up.

150g semolina
275ml milk
275ml water
pinch of grated nutmeg
2 eggs
30g Parmesan, pecorino or other cheese, grated
2 tsp olive oil

Preparation time: 25 minutes plus 1 hour in the fridge and 30 minutes cooking.
Equipment: 1 saucepan, 1 baking tray (about 20cm × 25cm) and 1 casserole dish.

Storage: Best eaten straight away, but otherwise fridge for 24 hours or freeze. Reheat under the grill or in the oven.
Servings: 2 adults and 1 baby or 10–12 baby portions.

- Prepare the ingredients by finely grating the cheese, beating the eggs in a cup or bowl and brushing oil over the baking tray.
- Put the milk, water and nutmeg into a pan and slowly add the semolina, stirring all the time.
- Bring to the boil, then cook for 5 minutes, still stirring constantly. The semolina should be bubbling a little all the time and should thicken and come away from the sides of the pan.
- Take the pan off the heat and stir in the eggs and most of the cheese.
- Pour the mixture into the baking tray and smooth over. Leave to cool slightly, then place in the fridge for about an hour until set. If you want to leave it for longer, that's fine.
- Preheat the oven to 200°C/400°F/gas mark 6.
- Take the mixture out of the fridge and cut it into pieces. You can cut it into circles with a pastry cutter or glass, or into slices like toast soldiers.
- Brush oil inside the casserole dish, then arrange the pieces. Start at one end and overlap them so that they look a bit like dominoes that have fallen down.
- Drizzle or brush the remaining oil over the top and sprinkle over the remaining cheese.
- Place in the oven for 30 minutes, until golden brown.

Bubble and squeak cakes

These are easy to make and can be eaten with meat, fish, eggs or just about anything.

1 tbsp rapeseed oil
2 large baking potatoes
¼ savoy or green cabbage
3 spring onions
25g plain flour

Preparation time: 40 minutes.
Equipment: 1 saucepan and 1 frying pan.
Storage: Fridge for 1–2 days or freeze. Reheat under the grill or in the oven.
Servings: 8 cakes for 2 adults and 1 baby, or 8 baby portions.

- Peel and chop the potatoes, then place them in the pan with enough water to cover them.
- Bring to the boil and simmer for 10–15 minutes until soft.
- Meanwhile, cut the cabbage and spring onions into very fine shreds.
- Heat half the oil in the frying pan and cook the cabbage and onion on a medium heat for 3–4 minutes until starting to soften.
- When the potatoes are cooked, drain them and leave the lid off the pan so that as much water as possible can evaporate.
- Mash the potatoes and stir in the cabbage mixture. Leave the frying pan to one side for now.
- Divide the mixture into eight portions, then, using your hands, form these into patties.
- Put the frying pan on a medium heat and add the remaining oil. Cook the potato cakes for about 4–5 minutes on each side until nicely browned.

Tips

- To make it more of a meal on its own, you can add an egg or some cheese to the mixture before cooking.
- If you have leftover Brussels sprouts or other cooked vegetables you can add these to the mixture too.

Celeriac champ

Celeriac isn't used very much in the UK and it certainly wouldn't win a beauty contest, but if you haven't tried it before you might be pleasantly surprised. It's good for family meals with a meaty stew or grilled salmon. It's also a great weaning food as it's easy to prepare, packed with antioxidants and introduces babies to a new flavour.

1 small celeriac
3 spring onions (or a few chives)
1 large potato
150ml milk
1 tbsp butter or margarine
black pepper (optional)

Preparation time: 30 minutes.
Equipment: 2 saucepans and 1 hand-held blender.
Storage: Fridge for 1–2 days or freeze.
Servings: 2 adults and 1 baby, or 12 baby portions.

- Peel and chop the potato, place the pieces in one of the pans and cover with water. Bring to the boil and simmer for 10–15 minutes until soft.
- Taking a good strong knife (celeriac is tough), cut off the root end. Then cut off chunks and cut the peel off. Dice the chunks into 1–1½cm cubes.
- Finely chop the spring onions or snip the chives.
- Place the celeriac, spring onion (or chives) and milk in the second pan. Bring to the boil and simmer gently for 5–10 minutes until soft.
- Drain the potato pieces and add them to the celeriac along with the butter or margarine. Whizz with a hand-held blender to make a creamy purée.

Tips

- Babies can have this for lunch mixed with peas and salmon or a little grated cheese.
- To make a dairy-free version, use water, soya milk or your baby's usual milk and dairy-free margarine.

Yorkshire pudding

This is great with a Sunday roast, of course, but you can also serve it with other foods, and babies can have leftovers instead of bread. Plus, it's easy to gum if you don't have any teeth.

80g plain flour
1 egg
75ml milk
25ml water
1 tbsp rapeseed oil

Preparation time: 10 minutes plus 20 minutes cooking.
Equipment: 1 small roasting tin, 1 mixing bowl and a wire or electric whisk.
Storage: Fridge for 1–2 days.
Servings: 2 adults and 2 babies.

- Preheat the oven to 220°C/425°F/gas mark 7.
- Put the flour in the mixing bowl. Make a well in the centre and crack the egg in.
- Beat the egg, then pour in the milk and water.
- Using a wire whisk or electric whisk, start whisking the liquid and slowly bring in the flour until you have a smooth, bubbly batter.

- Coat the roasting tin with the oil and place in the oven for a few minutes.
- Take the tin out of the oven and put it on the hob so that it gets smoking hot. Pour in the batter.
- Place the roasting tin on the top shelf of the oven for 20 minutes, until the Yorkshire pudding is golden brown and well risen.

Tips

- According to experts such as Delia and Jamie, the secret to a successful Yorkshire pudding is to make sure the tin is smoking hot before you begin and that you don't open the oven door while it's cooking.
- Some people prefer to rest the batter for between 15 minutes and eight hours before baking, but others say this makes no difference.

Puddings and snacks

Plain fruit or fruit and natural yogurt make excellent puddings and the recipes here provide a nice change as well as introducing flavours you might not have thought of. Snacks are important for babies to see them through between meals and it's a good idea to give a variety of plain or savoury foods rather than just sweet ones.

Nutty apple crumble

This is a twist on a traditional dish, making it really tasty and bursting with antioxidants, particularly selenium and vitamin E.

4 large cooking apples
75ml orange juice
50g self-raising flour
50g oats
35g margarine
20g demerara sugar
10g pumpkin seeds
30g nuts (e.g. Brazil nuts, walnuts, almonds)

Preparation time: 25 minutes plus 30 minutes cooking.
Equipment: 1 saucepan, 1 mixing bowl and 1 ovenproof dish.
Storage: Fridge for 1–2 days or freeze.
Servings: 2 adults and 1 baby.

- Preheat the oven to 200°C/400°F/gas mark 6.
- Quarter the apples, peel and core them, then cut them into chunks.
- Put the apple chunks and orange juice in the pan, bring to the boil and simmer for 5 minutes, until the apple is starting to soften.
- Meanwhile, put the flour and oats into a bowl and rub in the margarine with your fingers until the mixture resembles breadcrumbs.
- Put the nuts and seeds on a chopping board and chop quite finely.
- Mix the sugar, nuts and seeds into the flour mixture.
- Transfer the stewed apple into the ovenproof dish. Spoon the flour and nut mixture over the top and press down.
- Place in the oven for 30 minutes until nicely browned.

Tips

- Instead of using apples you could use 1kg of plums or rhubarb, or use a mixture of pears and forest fruits.
- The crumble can be served with ice cream or custard. Alternatively, make your own creamy topping by mixing 75g of ricotta with a teaspoon of soft brown sugar and a few drops of vanilla essence.

Mango and coconut rice

This is a quick and easy version of the traditional Thai dessert.

75g rice (sticky, fragrant Thai or basmati)
300ml water
2 whole cardamom pods
1 tsp caster sugar
20g coconut cream block
1 ripe mango

Preparation time: 10 minutes plus 12–15 minutes simmering.
Equipment: 1 saucepan.
Storage: Fridge for 24 hours or freeze.
Servings: 2 adult and 1 baby, or 10–12 baby portions.

- Put the rice, water and cardamom pods in a pan.
- Bring to the boil, cover and simmer until the rice is cooked but there is still some water in the pan, then turn off the heat.

- Grate the creamed coconut into the pan, add the sugar and stir. Put the lid back on the pan and leave for a few minutes until the remaining water has been absorbed.
- Meanwhile, remove the mango from its skin (p51) and dice.
- Remove the cardamom pods from the rice, and mix the mango with the rice.

Tips

- This can be eaten warm or cold.
- Babies who want to feed themselves can be given a slice of mango (with or without skin) and cooled rice, which becomes firmer and easier to handle.
- If you're reheating the rice to spoon-feed your baby, you might want to mix in a little water or milk.
- If you don't have a mango, try mashed or sliced banana instead.
- According to Allergy UK, coconuts are technically seeds rather than nuts and the majority of nut-allergic individuals can eat them. However, if this is an issue for you, you may want to talk to your doctor.

66 *This was delicious. We all loved it and it was so easy to make.* 99
Suzie, mum to Grace, 16 months

Chocolate rice pudding

This provides the antioxidant benefits of cocoa without all the saturated fat and sugar found in chocolate.

150g pudding rice
150ml water
650ml milk
2 tbsp sugar
1 tbsp cocoa
1 tsp vanilla extract

Preparation time: 15 minutes plus 25 minutes cooking.
Equipment: 1 saucepan.
Storage: Fridge for 1–2 days or freeze.
Servings: 8–10 baby portions.

- Bring the rice and water to the boil and simmer for about 5 minutes, until the water has been absorbed.
- Take the pan off the heat and stir in the other ingredients.
- Bring the mixture back to the boil and simmer for about 25 minutes, stirring occasionally.

Tips

- Serve slightly warm with sliced or mashed banana.
- Add extra milk if the pudding seems too thick.
- Purée slightly with a blender if necessary.

Apricot rice pudding

A lovely warming pudding sweetened with apricots, which also provide iron and beta-carotene.

125g pudding rice
150ml water
600ml milk
6 dried apricots
25g sultanas or dried mixed fruit
½ tsp mixed spice

Preparation time: 15 minutes plus 20 minutes cooking.
Equipment: 1 saucepan.
Storage: Fridge for 1–2 days or freeze.
Servings: 2 adults and 2 babies or 10–12 baby portions.

- Chop the apricots and place them in the pan with the rice, water and sultanas.
- Bring to the boil and simmer for about 5 minutes, until the water has been absorbed.
- Add the milk and mixed spice.
- Bring the mixture back to the boil and simmer for 20 minutes with the lid on, stirring occasionally.
- Leave to rest for a further 10 minutes with the lid on, then divide into portions.

Tips

- If the pudding is too thick, just stir in some extra milk.
- Purée slightly with a blender if needed.

Tropical fruit salad

These fruits can all be given to your baby raw to eat with her hands or they can be puréed and eaten fresh. However, making a batch of this delicious dessert is ideal for days when there's less time and you don't have such exciting fruit in the fruit bowl.

½ fresh pineapple
½ ripe mango
2 peaches or nectarines
1 medium banana
100ml apple juice, orange juice or water
40g couscous

Preparation time: 15 minutes plus 5 minutes cooking.
Equipment: 1 saucepan and 1 food processor or hand-held blender.
Storage: Fridge for 1–2 days or freeze.
Servings: 6–8 baby portions.

- Cut the skin off the pineapple and remove any 'eyes'. Cut into quarters, then cut out the woody core. Dice the flesh into pieces no bigger than 1cm cubes.
- Remove the mango from its skin (p51) and dice.
- Remove the skin from the peaches or nectarines, then cut the flesh off the stone and dice.
- Place the pineapple, mango and peach in a pan with the juice or water.
- Bring to the boil, then slice the banana into the pan and simmer with the lid on for 5 minutes.
- Add the couscous and stir, then turn off the heat and leave for 5–10 minutes with the lid on while the couscous absorbs the fruit juices.
- Using a food processor or a hand-held blender, give a few pulses to make a coarse purée.

Tips

- If you taste this while it's still hot it will be tart, but it seems sweeter when cooled.

Cheese and tomato scone biscuits

These have a mild flavour and are like a very thin scone, which means they're soft enough to eat without teeth but solid enough not to turn to mush or fall apart too easily. They freeze well so you can just defrost one or two at a time.

150g plain flour
50g wholemeal flour
2 tsp baking powder
50g Cheddar cheese, grated
1 tbsp tomato purée
2 tbsp rapeseed oil
1 egg and 50–75ml milk, or 100–125ml milk

Preparation time: 15 minutes plus 10 minutes cooking.
Equipment: 2 baking trays and 1 mixing bowl.
Storage: Airtight container for 2–3 days or freeze.
Servings: 30 biscuits.

- Preheat the oven to 200°C/400°F/gas mark 6.
- Mix together the flour, baking powder and grated cheese.
- Stir in the tomato purée, oil and an egg if you're using one.
- Add as much milk as is needed to make a dough.
- Using your hands, bring the dough together to form a ball.
- Place the dough on a floured work surface and roll it to a thickness of 5–7mm.
- Cut it into circles 5cm across using a biscuit cutter, or into fingers if you prefer.
- Place the biscuits on a lightly baking tray and bake for 10 minutes.

Chocolate and Brazil nut scone biscuits

Brazil nuts are the best source of selenium around, which is important for your baby's developing immune system. Here they're combined with cocoa to provide even more antioxidants, but also a lovely flavour.

200g plain flour
2 tsp baking powder
2 tbsp cocoa powder

2 tbsp caster sugar
50g Brazil nuts
75ml rapeseed oil
1 egg (beaten) and 25ml milk, or 100ml milk

Preparation time: 15 minutes plus 10 minutes cooking.
Equipment: 2 baking trays, 1 mixing bowl and 1 food processor.
Storage: Airtight container for 2–3 days or freeze.
Servings: 30–35 biscuits.

- Preheat the oven to 190°C/375°F/gas mark 5.
- Mix together the flour, baking powder, sifted cocoa powder and sugar.
- Put the nuts in a food processor to grind them or finely chop with a chopping knife and then add them to the flour mixture.
- Add the oil, egg (if using) and milk and stir well to combine the ingredients into a lumpy paste.
- Using your hands, bring the dough together to form a ball.
- Place the dough on a floured work surface and roll it out to a thickness of about ½cm.
- Cut the dough into circles 5cm across using a biscuit cutter, or into fingers if you prefer.
- Place the biscuits on a lightly baking tray and bake for 10 minutes.

Tips

- Brazil nuts are very hard, so for small babies it's best to grind them completely to make them easier to eat and digest.
- For a nut-free version, just leave the nuts out or replace them with dried fruit.

Cheesy corn muffins

These are lovely for lunch straight from the oven.

100g fine cornmeal
100g plain flour
2 tsp baking powder
75g Cheddar cheese
1 tbsp rapeseed oil, plus extra for greasing
1 egg
150ml milk

Preparation time: 10 minutes plus 10–15 minutes cooking.
Equipment: 1 muffin tin and 1 mixing bowl.
Storage: Airtight container for 2–3 days or freeze.
Servings: 12 muffins.

- Preheat the oven to 200°C/400°F/gas mark 6.
- Grease the muffin tin.
- Mix the dry ingredients in the bowl, then grate in the cheese and mix.
- Make a well in the centre of the mixture and add the oil, egg and milk. Beat with a fork, then bring in the dry ingredients from the sides of the bowl and mix well.
- Spoon the mixture into the muffin tin and bake for 10–15 minutes until nicely browned.
- Leave the muffins to cool in the tin for a few minutes, then place them on a wire cooling rack.

Tips

- Cornmeal is not the same thing as cornflour, which is used for making gravy or custard. It is available from most supermarkets and you might find it with Caribbean foods.
- These make a good snack, or have them for lunch with vegetable sticks and houmous or another dip.

> 66 *I made these as a post-nursery snack and we both really enjoyed them.* 99
> **Emma, mum to Daisy, 11 months**

Choconana buns

These get all their sweetness from bananas and they are easy for babies to eat as well as being popular with older children.

4 medium ripe bananas, mashed
2 eggs, lightly beaten
100ml rapeseed oil, plus extra for greasing
175g self-raising flour
1 tbsp cocoa

Preparation time: 15 minutes plus 10–15 minutes cooking.
Equipment: 2 fairy cake/muffin tins and 1 mixing bowl.

Storage: Airtight container for 3–4 days or freeze.
Servings: 16–24 buns.

- Preheat the oven to 200°C/400°F/gas mark 6.
- Grease your tins or put cupcake cases in the holes.
- Mix together the bananas, oil and eggs.
- Sift the flour and cocoa into the bowl and stir to combine all the ingredients.
- Spoon the mixture into the bun tin.
- Bake for 10–15 minutes, until well risen and firm to the touch.
- Cool for a few minutes in the bun tin, then turn out on to a wire rack to finishing cooling.

Tips

- You can make the buns as big or small as you like. Bigger buns are good for sharing or you can fill two whole fairy cake tins and make 24 baby-sized buns.

> ❝ I made these with gluten-free flour (I'm a coeliac) and both Sophie and I enjoyed them. She's both dairy-free and an incredibly picky eater, and hasn't liked the dairy-free cakes I've cooked previously, but these were really moist and light. ❞
> **Charlie, mum to Sophie, 3 years, and Olivia, 6 months**

Healthy snacks

- Breadsticks
- Rice cakes
- Fingers of toast, pitta or chapatti
- Cooked vegetable sticks
- Cold cooked potato
- Small cubes or sticks of cheese
- Half a banana
- Pieces of fruit

Meal plan for a 7- to 9-month-old baby

The five-day meal plan below shows how a 7 to 9-month-old baby can meet all her nutrient requirements from three meals and two snacks a day, alongside three or four breastfeeds or 500–600ml of infant formula. In general, babies this age have three milk feeds a day: first thing in the morning, mid-afternoon and at bedtime. Your baby should also have a cup of water to drink with each meal and snack. The meal plan isn't meant to be followed strictly but it shows what a healthy diet for a baby this age looks like.

Day	Breakfast	Snack	Lunch	Snack	Dinner
1	Eggy bread soldiers (p66) Cherry tomatoes (halved)	Rice cakes	Macaroni cheese (p80) with green beans	Chocolate and Brazil nut scone biscuit (p100)	Lamb shank with tomato and rosemary (p90), celeriac champ (p93) and steamed carrot sticks Half a raw peach
2	Ready Brek with milk Half a banana	Leftover steamed carrot sticks	Leftover celeriac champ (p93) with mashed sardine and broccoli spears Strawberries	Mini breadsticks	Baked aubergine and lentils (p76) with rice Slice of melon
3	Polenta pancakes (p27) Apple, apricot and banana (p53)	Raisins	Leftover polenta pancakes (p27) with houmous, leftover baked aubergine and lentils (p76) Apple purée with yogurt	Rice cakes	Pasta with chicken and broccoli (p87) Jar of fruity yogurt

| 4 | Weetabix with milk Half a kiwi | Rice cakes with smooth peanut butter | Leftover pasta with salmon pâté (p67) and cherry tomatoes (halved) | ½ a pear | Lentil and vegetable cobbler (p78) Mango and coconut rice (p96) |
| 5 | Fruit and nut porridge (p65) or porridge fingers (p26) | Dried apricots | Houmous and avocado on toast with green beans Strawberries | Breadsticks | Fish and tomato pie (p84) with broccoli Half a banana |

This meal plan meets the requirements for energy, protein, potassium, calcium, magnesium, phosphorus, iron, copper, zinc, chloride, selenium, iodine, thiamin, riboflavin, niacin, folic acid and vitamins A, B6, B12, C, D and E. It also contains less than 1g of salt per day, which is the maximum babies should have.

This meal plan is practical to prepare and good for your baby's health and development as it includes the following:

- both finger foods and mashed foods at most meals
- homemade family meals that are suitable for babies, such as fish and tomato pie (if you eat later than your baby, then she could have these for lunch the following day)
- no rusks or snack foods with added flavourings
- only two slices of bread over the five days, as more would have resulted in a higher salt intake than recommended
- only convenience foods that are suitable for babies, such as low salt fortified breakfast cereals and a jar of baby dessert
- simple meals and snacks that include leftover pasta or vegetables
- meat no more than every other day, and fish or vegetarian meals on other days instead.

Dos, don'ts and FAQs for your 7- to 9-month-old

Do

- Establish a pattern of three regular meals a day.
- Give finger foods every day or ideally give them at every meal.
- Introduce lots of different foods and textures, including fish and a variety of vegetables.
- Help your baby to eat with a spoon if she needs it and wants it.
- Check fish carefully for bones.
- Take a flexible approach with spoons and finger foods to suit your baby's mood and the food you're offering.

Don't

- Purée all your baby's meals to make them smooth.
- Give your baby more than 500–600ml milk per day or three or four breastfeeds.
- Worry if your baby doesn't finish what you give her.
- Limit your baby's diet because you want to do BLW and your baby can't manage sloppy foods (e.g. porridge) herself. A bit of spoon-loading or spoon-feeding is fine.
- Rush your baby during meals – if time is limited give foods that are easier to eat.

FAQs

Q: My baby gags on anything apart from a really smooth purée. Should I just stick with purées for now?

A: The short answer is no, for several reasons. Firstly, gagging may look alarming but it's different to choking and your baby will learn to cope with lumps (p17). So be vigilant but don't show your concern or this will reinforce the idea that lumps are a problem. Since she gags even on tiny lumps this may seem odd, but giving finger foods may also help. Smooth purées can almost be drunk but if you give her something like a rice cake she can slowly nibble a piece off, feel it on her lips and at the front of her mouth and learn about chewing.

It's not a good idea to wait before giving lumps, as there appears to be a 'window of opportunity' between 6 and 9 months when babies are more likely to start accepting them. Research has shown that babies who aren't given lumpy food at this age are more likely to have feeding problems and be fussy eaters later on. As well as introducing finger foods you can try puréeing her food just a fraction less, so that it doesn't have big lumps but just a bit of texture. Try it with something she really enjoys eating and gradually purée it less and less until you can just mash it with a fork or give it as it is.

Q: How can I get my baby to eat savoury foods? She just wants to have pudding.

A: Babies have a naturally sweet tooth so this can be tricky. The first thing to do is make sure the puddings she's having are as healthy as possible, for example pure fruit purées, natural yogurt or a mixture. It's best to avoid puddings with added sugar – even some flavoured yogurts or fromage frais can be very sweet. At snack time avoid giving sweet snacks such as rusks or biscuits and instead give her plain rice cakes or other healthy snacks (p103). You can also try giving pieces of cooked carrot or cold potato as a snack.

Also, make sure you keep offering vegetables and savoury foods at lunch and dinner every day. This can seem a waste of time if it's hardly eaten but it's important to persevere. You can offer sweeter vegetables such as parsnips and squash or mix in some fruit. Manufacturers do this and some pouches of spinach or broccoli actually contain more fruit than vegetable, but this isn't a long-term solution. It can be a useful way to start though, if you then gradually reduce the amount of fruit used. Ultimately, the more often your baby tastes a particular food the more likely she is to eat it and enjoy it – so keep going.

Q: At breakfast time, my baby doesn't seem hungry. What should I do?

A: Check that your baby isn't having too much milk first thing in the morning (p12) and remember that milk added to cereal also counts towards your baby's daily milk requirements. Also, if she tends to have breakfast immediately, it might be better to wait, maybe for an hour, for the milk to be digested.

Of course, some babies, like some adults, can't seem to face food in the morning, in which case make sure you have something nutritious for her to eat later, especially if you're going out. The danger for breakfast-dodgers is that they have less nutritious snacks instead, such as biscuits. Keep offering her breakfast, but maybe keep back some of it for later. Something like eggy bread soldiers (p66) can be eaten cold later, or give her some fruit, oatcakes or blueberry breakfast cake (p159).

Q: How can I get my baby to eat faster?

A: Some babies are just naturally slower eaters and there's little you can do, so try to allow your baby the time she needs and don't cut meals short before she's had enough. Try to minimise distractions at mealtimes such as TV, other children playing or adults doing other things. Sitting down with your baby will also encourage her to focus on the food.

If you're trying BLW, it could be that she doesn't have the skills to eat any faster yet and needs you to help her with a spoon for now. Practice will also help – when there's time, give her the opportunity to explore and play with her food as much as she wants to. Also, think about the types of foods you're giving her. Try something like porridge fingers and fruit for breakfast when there's time, and porridge on busier mornings.

Q: My baby now refuses to be spoon-fed. How do I make sure she gets all the different foods she needs via finger foods?

A: Around this age some babies start to gain 'independence' and refuse to be spoon-fed. If you keep trying you could end up with a real battle on your hands, so it's much better to go along with this. With careful planning it's possible to give finger foods from all the food groups. Fruit and vegetables tend to be the easiest for babies to feed themselves, as they can have pieces of roast or steamed vegetables (p35) and pieces of raw fruit (p56). Starchy carbohydrates are slightly more difficult, but well-cooked pasta and pieces of potato are good, or you can make pancakes or finger foods such as leek and pea patties (p116) that include flour.

Protein foods such as meat and fish are probably the trickiest for babies to handle when they have few teeth and limited skills. Some enjoy a chicken drumstick (without skin), or try chicken and vegetable fingers (p48). Fish and beans can be included in pâtés or dips, and eggs can be eaten as pieces of omelette or tortilla. Your baby may not eat certain foods some days, but if you offer a protein food, some starchy carbs and vegetables or fruit at every meal, then things should balance out over a few days. Also, don't be limited by what you think of as finger foods. You might be surprised at how well your child manages with family meals such as pasta or chunky soup.

4 Feeding your 10- to 12-month-old

As your baby approaches her first birthday she's likely to become a much more confident and capable diner. Make the most of it now, because toddlers often become fussier as they get older. Use this period to introduce as many new foods as possible, with a variety from each food group. Even if she seems to love pasta, for example, try not to give it to her every day. There is a range of alternatives, including rice, couscous, polenta and potato. Likewise, give her lots of different-coloured vegetables and fruit: yellow, orange, green, purple and red. And even if you've got a confirmed meat-eater in the house, try to have fish a couple of times a week, and meat-free dishes with beans or lentils some days too. It is also good to vary the way you cook particular foods; for example, fish can be eaten grilled, or eaten in stews, pasta sauces and dips. While meals should be varied and imaginative, it is best to eat them at regular times. If your baby has a firmly established routine of three meals and two small snacks a day, then it will be much easier to keep her on track in the future.

Now is a good time to start encouraging your baby to feed herself with a spoon and fork. This is true both for those who started off being mainly spoon-fed and those who've always eaten with their fingers. It takes a while to learn how to use cutlery and it's fine if your baby still eats some things with her hands, but mastering a spoon will mean she can handle a greater variety of foods, such as porridge or bolognese. As your baby becomes better able to feed herself and more sociable, it becomes easier to eat together and have the same foods. Sharing meals is very beneficial for babies. It also encourages everyone in the family to eat more healthily, since babies can't have processed foods such as sausages or ready meals. Although babies can eat most foods at this age you still need to be careful about a few, particularly those with lots of salt (p15).

Daily requirements for 10- to 12-month-old babies

Each day, try to offer your baby:

- 3–4 servings of starchy foods (e.g. bread, pasta, potatoes)
- 3–4 servings of fruit and vegetables (different colours if possible)
- 2 servings of meat, fish, eggs, tofu, lentils or other pulses
- 3–4 breastfeeds or 500–600ml of formula.

Breakfasts

The breakfast ideas suggested in the last chapter are all still good for your baby now. If she will only eat with her hands, then porridge fingers (p26) and pancakes could be the answer. Or try a Weetabix-type cereal with just a small amount of milk. This makes it easier for babies to pick it up with their hands, or with a spoon when they can manage it. The extra iron and vitamins in cereals can make a big difference to the micronutrient intake of babies so it's good to have them if at all possible.

Scotch pancakes

These are also known as drop scones and are much easier for babies to eat than thin crêpe-type pancakes. The exact quantities of ingredients aren't too important so you really can't go wrong, and it's easy to adapt the recipe according to your baby's needs.

200g plain white flour (or 100g white and 100g wholemeal)
1 tsp baking powder
2 eggs
225ml whole milk
rapeseed oil

Preparation time: 20 minutes.
Equipment: 1 frying pan and 1 mixing bowl.
Storage: Best eaten straight away, or fridge for 24 hours or freeze, separated by sheets of greaseproof paper. Reheat in the oven or under the grill.

Servings: 18 pancakes – babies might eat 1 or 2.

- Put the flour and baking powder into the bowl.
- Make a well in the centre, crack the eggs into it and pour in the milk. Beat with a fork, wire whisk or electric whisk until smooth.
- Heat a small amount of oil in the frying pan, then drop in a tablespoon of the mixture. It will spread out slightly but you should be able to make six pancakes at a time.
- When the edges look set and small bubbles appear on the surface of the pancake, flip it over with a spatula or fish slice and cook the other side. Each side takes 1 or 2 minutes to cook.

Tips

- Give these to your baby with fresh fruit, fruit compote, purée or yogurt.
- To make oaty pancakes, substitute half the flour with oats and use slightly more milk (250ml).
- To make gluten-free scotch pancakes, use 200g gluten-free flour or make polenta pancakes (p27). For an egg-free recipe try banana pancakes (p28).

Apple and sultana overnight muesli

It's easy to eat the same thing every morning, but if you spend a few minutes making this in the evening you can wake up to a healthy breakfast that's ready to go straight from the fridge or popped in the microwave for a minute or two.

60g porridge oats
1 medium apple
1 tbsp sultanas
250ml milk
2 tbsp natural yogurt

Preparation time: 5 minutes plus overnight soaking.
Equipment: 1 bowl.
Storage: Best eaten within 24 hours.
Servings: 1 adult and 1 baby.

- Weigh the oats and sultanas into a bowl or plastic tub.
- Peel, core and finely grate the apple into the oat mixture.

- Pour on the milk and give it a stir, then cover with cling film or a lid and put it in the fridge overnight.
- In the morning, give it a stir, then put it into bowls and add a big dollop of yogurt.

Tips

- For older children there is no need to peel the apple.
- You can add other dried fruit or chopped nuts to the mixture, such as hazelnuts or Brazil nuts.
- Brighten it up by adding some sliced strawberries or other berries in the morning, or a spoonful of fruit purée.
- If your baby finds it too cold straight from the fridge, you can put it in the microwave to take the chill off, then give it a good stir.

> 66 *I zapped this in the microwave for 90 seconds in the morning. It was delicious and we both enjoyed it.* 99
> **Emma, mum to Elizabeth, 14 months**

Breakfast couscous

A warm and satisfying breakfast that will set you up for the day and provide one of your five a day. It's even easier to make than porridge as you don't need to stir it while it cooks, and it may appeal to those who find porridge a bit gluey.

200ml milk
3 dates
2 tsp sultanas
pinch of cinnamon
50g couscous

Preparation time: 5 minutes plus 5 minutes soaking.
Equipment: 1 saucepan.
Storage: Fridge for 1–2 days or freeze.
Servings: 1 adult and 1 baby.

- Put the milk in a pan and place it on a medium heat.
- While it's warming, chop the dates and add them to the milk, along with the sultanas and cinnamon.

- When the milk starts to bubble, stir in the couscous, turn off the heat and put a lid on the pan.
- Leave for 5 minutes while the couscous absorbs the milk, then stir and serve. Sprinkle a little more cinnamon on top if wanted.

Tips

- Experiment with other dried fruit such as apricots, raisins or prunes. You can also add some chopped nuts, such as hazelnuts or Brazil nuts.
- If your baby wants to eat this with her hands, you might want to use a little less milk so that it's less runny.
- If you just want to make a portion for your baby, heat up some milk in a bowl using the microwave, then add the other ingredients and cover with a small plate. You'll need approximately one part couscous to four parts milk.
- Couscous is wheat-based and therefore contains gluten, but you can buy gluten-free versions made from rice or corn.

Lunches and dinners

Sandwiches and toast fingers make easy lunches, but try to avoid giving them to your baby every day. One slice of bread provides 0.5g salt, which is half the maximum amount your baby should have in a day. Instead, leftover pasta or other foods from your evening meal are better, lower salt options. Finger foods and dips are also popular with babies this age.

Finger foods for dipping
- Scotch pancakes (p111)
- Toast fingers or strips of pitta bread
- Breadsticks
- Rice cakes
- Polenta pancakes (p27)
- Pieces of corn flatbread or wrap (p70)
- Potato wedges or oven chips
- Vegetable sticks or pieces
- Potato farls (p140)
- Leek and pea patties (p116)
- Baked courgette fingers (p73)
- Peanut butter burgers (p119)

- Chickpea and rice batons (p115)
- Falafel (p75)
- Pieces of meat or chicken (p89)
- Sage and onion sausage (p135)
- Chicken and vegetable fingers (p48)
- Tuna meatballs (p174)
- Salmon and spring onion rösti (p175)
- Salmon and oat patties (p132)

Dips

- Houmous
- Soya bean and pea houmous (p69)
- Guacamole
- Avocado and yogurt dip (p43)
- Beetroot dip (p120)
- Beany dip (p120)
- Homemade ketchup (p183) mixed with some yogurt
- Lentil dhal (pp44 and 78)
- Vegetable purée
- Mushy peas (p141)
- Soup (pp72 and 122)
- Cheese sauce
- Fruit purée
- Purées made with meat, chicken or fish

Many of the spreads and fillings on p164 can also be made runnier for dipping if you add a little water, stock, milk or yogurt.

Chickpea and rice batons

These are good for babies to feed themselves as they're fairly soft but don't break up too easily.

100g basmati or other long-grain rice
1 × 400g tin chickpeas
1 onion

> 1 garlic clove (optional)
> ¼ tsp ground coriander
> ¼ tsp sweet paprika
> 1 egg yolk
> 1 tbsp tomato purée
> 1–2 tsp olive or rapeseed oil

Preparation time: 25 minutes plus 20 minutes cooking.
Equipment: 1 saucepan, 1 mixing bowl, 1 baking tray and 1 food processor or hand-held blender.
Storage: Fridge for 1–2 days or freeze. Reheat in the oven.
Servings: 15–20 batons depending on size.

- Cook the rice with about 250ml of water or according to the instructions on the packet.
- Brush the oil over the baking tray and preheat the oven to 180°C/350°F/ gas mark 4.
- Drain the chickpeas and place them in the mixing bowl.
- Finely dice the onion and crush the garlic, then add these to the chickpeas.
- Add the spices, tomato purée and egg yolk, and purée the mixture until fairly smooth.
- When the rice is cooked, mix it thoroughly with the other ingredients using a fork.
- Take walnut-sized pieces of the mixture and roll into batons. You can make these thicker like sausages, or thinner, more like breadsticks, whichever suits your baby.
- Place the batons on the baking tray, brush with a little more oil and bake for 20 minutes.

Tips

- These freeze well and can be defrosted and reheated in the oven for 5–10 minutes.
- Serve with a dip such as houmous, avocado and yogurt dip (p43) or mushy peas (p141).

Leek and pea patties

These make a fairly balanced meal all on their own as they contain vegetables, starchy carbs and eggs for protein. They also go well with a dip and veggie sticks. They freeze very well too and can be eaten when you're out without creating too much mess.

1–2 tbsp olive or rapeseed oil
1 large or 2 small leeks
125g frozen peas
3 mint leaves (optional)
2 eggs
50g plain flour
50g wholemeal flour
1 tsp baking powder

Preparation time: 30 minutes.
Equipment: 1 frying pan and 1 mixing bowl.
Storage: Fridge for 24 hours or freeze.
Servings: 14–18 patties – babies might eat 1 or 2 depending on their appetite and if they're having other foods with them.

- Cut the leek in quarters lengthways and check that it's clean all the way through.
- Finely slice the leek. Discard some of the green parts if they are tough, but some green is fine.
- Heat two teaspoons of oil in the frying pan and gently fry the leek for about 5 minutes, until soft.
- Meanwhile, put the plain flour, wholemeal flour, baking powder and eggs in a mixing bowl. Mix together well using a fork.
- Finely chop the mint and add it to the pan, along with the peas. Continue to cook for 2–3 minutes.
- Transfer the leek and pea mixture to the mixing bowl and set aside the pan for a minute.
- Mix all the ingredients thoroughly. You can do this quite roughly so that the peas get popped, as this makes them easier for babies to digest.
- Heat another teaspoon of oil in the pan and drop one heaped tablespoon of mixture per patty into the pan. You should be able to cook four or five at a time. Press the mixture down slightly with the back of your spoon so that it's no more than 1½cm thick.
- Cook for 1 minute on each side, until browned.

Tips

- Add some garlic and shallots for extra flavour.
- Try making these with different vegetables, such as broccoli, courgette, chopped beans or mashed sweetcorn.
- These go well with a dip such as houmous or avocado and yogurt dip (p43).

❝ *These were great. I found a smaller patty was easier for Izzy. She picked it up and ate a fair portion. It's a good introduction to bigger bits that she can pick up and eat herself.* **❞**
Carolyn, mum to Isla, 4 years, Rowan, 2 years, and Isobel, 10 months

Cauliflower pizza bites

These mini pizza bites have a base made from cauliflower and can be topped with cheese and tomato or your favourite topping. If your baby has turned her nose up at cauliflower in the past, this is well worth a try as the flavour is heavily disguised.

1 medium cauliflower
100g cream cheese
1 egg, beaten
2 tbsp tomato purée
30g Cheddar or mozzarella cheese, grated

Preparation time: 20 minutes plus 30 minutes cooking.
Equipment: 2 baking trays and 1 mixing bowl.
Storage: Fridge for 24 hours or freeze. Reheat under the grill or in the oven.
Servings: 14–16 pizza bites.

- Preheat the oven to 200°C/400°F/gas mark 6. Place a piece of greaseproof paper on each of the baking trays.
- Coarsely grate the cauliflower into the mixing bowl. Rather than cutting the cauliflower into pieces before grating, it's easiest if you start with the whole cauliflower and then throw away the stump that you're left with.
- Put the grated cauliflower, sometimes called 'cauliflower rice', into the microwave for 7–8 minutes.
- Take the cauliflower out of the microwave, give it a stir and leave it to steam for a couple of minutes.
- Add the cream cheese and beaten egg and stir.
- Take a heaped tablespoon of the mixture for each pizza. Place it on the baking tray and pat down to form a circle about 1cm thick and 6–7cm in diameter.
- Bake in the oven for 25 minutes, until slightly browned.
- Take the trays out of the oven and turn it up to 230°C/450°F/gas mark 8.

- Thinly spread a little tomato purée on each base and sprinkle grated cheese on top.
- Return the trays to the oven for 5 minutes, until the cheese is bubbling.
- Leave the pizza bites to cool for 5 minutes before using a fish slice to take them carefully off the greaseproof paper.

Tips

- If you want to freeze some of the pizza bites, it is best to do this once they are baked, but before the cheese and tomato topping is added.

Peanut butter burger

This isn't a Man v. Food*-type creation, with peanut butter on top of a mountainous beef burger, but a really easy light lunch for you and your baby to share. Have the burgers with salad and a little bread, or your baby could have mashed vegetables on the side.*

> 30g peanut butter (crunchy or smooth)
> 2 tbsp cream cheese
> 50g wholemeal or granary breadcrumbs
> 1 spring onion

Preparation time: 5 minutes plus 6–8 minutes cooking.
Equipment: 1 bowl.
Storage: Best eaten straight away.
Servings: 1 adult and 1 baby.

- Mix together the cream cheese and peanut butter.
- Finely chop the spring onion and turn the bread into breadcrumbs if not already crumbed.
- Mix the breadcrumbs and spring onion with the cream cheese and peanut butter mixture, then, using your hands, form the mixture into two burgers.
- Turn the grill on to medium and place a piece of foil on the grill tray to put the burgers on.
- Grill for 3–4 minutes on each side.

> 66 *These were a resounding success. We loved them and they got the thumbs up from the decidedly difficult one. A massive bonus is the nutritional value of peanut butter to a child who isn't a big fan of meat. Or fish for that matter.* 99
> **Claude, mum to Carys, 17 months**

Beetroot dip

An easy dip to prepare, which makes a nice change from houmous and has a fabulous colour.

1 × 400g tin chickpeas (or white beans)
250g cooked vacuum-packed beetroot (not pickled)
1 garlic clove, crushed
1 tbsp natural yogurt
1 tbsp olive oil
juice of ½ lemon
pinch of cumin (optional)

Preparation time: 10 minutes.
Equipment: 1 food processor or 1 deep-sided bowl and hand-held blender.
Storage: Fridge for 1–2 days or freeze.
Servings: 12–15 baby portions.

- Drain the chickpeas and place them in the food processor.
- Add all the other ingredients.
- Purée until smooth.

Tips

- If you want to prepare this with fresh beetroot, simply wash them, place them in a pan covered in water and boil until tender. Remove the skin once the beetroot has cooled, then use as described above.
- If your baby doesn't seem keen on this to start with, try mixing it with cream cheese to make it creamier and to give it a more familiar flavour.
- For a dairy-free version, leave out the yogurt or swap it for tahini.
- For an even easier dip, simply purée equal quantities of houmous and cooked beetroot. This also produces a smoother dip than you can achieve if you start with whole chickpeas.

Beany dip

This takes next to no time to prepare and doesn't need cooking. Also, you can adjust the recipe to suit your baby's taste.

1 × 400g tin kidney beans
½ × 400g tin chopped tomatoes
2 tbsp tomato purée
2 tbsp peanut butter (or tahini)
3 tbsp cream cheese
1 tbsp lemon juice
a few fresh basil leaves, chopped (optional)

Preparation time: 10 minutes.
Equipment: 1 food processor or 1 deep-sided bowl and hand-held blender.
Storage: Fridge for 1–2 days or freeze.
Servings: 12–15 baby portions.

- Drain the kidney beans and place them in the food processor.
- Add all the other ingredients.
- Purée until smooth.

Tips

- Serve with corn flatbread (p71) or pitta bread soldiers and some veggie sticks.
- If you want to make it thicker for spreading, rather than dipping, leave out the tinned tomato and use an extra spoonful of tomato purée instead.
- To make the dip suitable for those who can't eat dairy, replace the cream cheese with some butternut squash.
- If your baby can't have nuts, you can use tahini. If you're avoiding seeds too, then use extra cream cheese and basil.

Aubergine dip

This provides babies with a new taste and a novel texture that many seem to enjoy.

1 medium aubergine
1 tsp rapeseed or olive oil
½ onion
1 garlic clove, crushed (or more if you like)
2 tbsp fresh parsley, chopped
2 tbsp plain yogurt
1 tbsp lemon juice
pinch of paprika

Preparation time: 15 minutes plus 20 minutes cooking.
Equipment: 1 baking or roasting tin, 1 frying pan, and 1 food processor or 1 deep-sided bowl and hand-held blender.
Storage: Fridge for 1–2 days.
Servings: 1 pot (houmous sized).

- Preheat the oven to 200°C/400°F/gas mark 6.
- Cut the end off the aubergine and then cut it in half lengthways. Brush the cut sides with one teaspoon of oil and place in a roasting tin skin side down.
- Bake for 20 minutes, until the flesh starts to brown, then leave to cool slightly.
- Peel and dice the onion.
- Heat a teaspoonful of oil in a frying pan and sauté the onion with the crushed garlic for 5 minutes, until soft.
- Scrape the flesh from the aubergine into a bowl or food processor and discard the skin.
- Add the onion mixture, parsley, yogurt, lemon juice and paprika.
- Blend until smooth and eat warm or cold.

Tips

- If your baby doesn't seem keen on this to start with but likes houmous, mix the two together.
- Serve with warm pitta, wrap (p70) or corn flatbread (p71).

Red lentil soup

A thick, warming soup that takes less than half an hour to cook. It's just slightly spicy and tastes great with warm bread or cheesy corn muffins (p101).

1 tbsp olive oil
1 onion
2 medium carrots
125g red lentils
1 bay leaf
½ tsp mild curry powder
1 very low salt stock cube made up with 400ml water
1 × 400g tin chopped tomatoes

Preparation time: 10 minutes plus 20 minutes cooking.
Equipment: 1 saucepan and 1 hand-held blender.
Storage: Fridge for 1–2 days or freeze.
Servings: 2 adults and 2 children.

- Peel and dice the onion.
- Heat the oil in the pan and cook the onion with the lid on for 2–3 minutes so that it softens but doesn't brown.
- Peel the carrots, chop them in half lengthways and slice.
- Add the carrots, lentils, bay leaf and curry powder to the saucepan and mix.
- Pour in the stock, give it another stir and bring to the boil, then simmer for 10 minutes with the lid on.
- Add the chopped tomatoes and cook for another 5 minutes.
- Remove the bay leaf and use a hand-held blender to make the soup as smooth as you like.

Tips

- You can make the soup thicker if your baby would find it easier to eat that way or if you want to serve it with pasta. Simply add a couple of spoonfuls of tomato purée instead of chopped tomatoes.

Thick leek and potato soup

This simple soup can be adapted to include whatever vegetables you have to hand, or whichever vegetable you're struggling to include in your baby's diet.

1 tbsp olive oil
1 onion
2 leeks
2 potatoes
1 bay leaf
2 very low salt stock cubes made up with 600ml water
1 tbsp fresh parsley or 1 tsp dried parsley
pinch of ground nutmeg
½ tsp lemon juice
100–200ml milk

Preparation time: 20 minutes plus 20 minutes cooking.
Equipment: 1 saucepan.
Storage: Fridge for 1–2 days or freeze.
Servings: 2 adults and 2 children.

- Peel and dice the onion. Cut off the ends of the leek and discard, then cut the leek in half lengthways, give it an extra wash if needed, and slice thinly.

- Heat the oil in the pan and cook the onion and leek over a low heat with the lid on to sweat for 5 minutes, until softened but not browned.
- Meanwhile, peel the potatoes and dice into 1cm cubes.
- Add the potato to the pan and continue to sweat for a further 5 minutes.
- Add the stock, lemon juice, nutmeg, bay leaf and parsley to the pan. Bring to the boil with the lid on and simmer for about 5–10 minutes, until the potato is tender.
- Remove the bay leaf and use a hand-held blender to make the soup as smooth as you like.
- Stir in as much milk as you like to get a good consistency for your baby. Add freshly ground black pepper to taste (maybe just for adults).

Tips

- You can add any other vegetables you like, such as carrot, broccoli, courgette or butternut squash. Cut these like the potato and add at the same time.
- This soup can be turned into pea soup by adding a few handfuls of frozen peas when the potatoes are nearly ready.

Easy pasta and adzuki bean salad

This recipe turns leftover pasta into a nutritious lunch in just a few minutes. It can easily be adapted to make use of whatever you have in the fridge.

2–3 tbsp leftover pasta
1 tbsp tinned adzuki beans or other beans
1 tbsp houmous
1 tbsp natural yogurt
3 cherry tomatoes

Preparation time: 5 minutes.
Equipment: 1 bowl.
Storage: Eat straight away or fridge for 24 hours.
Servings: 1 baby.

- Cut the tomatoes in half or quarters.
- Mix all the ingredients together.
- Serve cold, or heated slightly if your baby prefers it warm.

Meals to make with leftover pasta

- Avocado, yogurt or cottage cheese, Cheddar and peas
- Houmous, yogurt and chopped tomato
- Tinned sardines mashed with homemade ketchup (p183)
- Mashed vegetables and cheese
- Tuna, avocado and grated cucumber
- Chicken, avocado and peas
- Mashed vegetables and peanut butter

Bean sausages

These are great for eating with your fingers and also make a good family meal with mash, carrots and gravy.

1 × 400g tin mixed beans
25g raisins
½ tsp ground cumin
2 tbsp peanut butter
1 tbsp tomato purée
25g oats
2 medium carrots
1 egg
75g wholemeal breadcrumbs
2 tsp rapeseed oil
a little plain flour

Preparation time: 20 minutes.
Equipment: 1 frying pan, 1 food processor or 1 deep-sided bowl and hand-held blender, 1 bowl and 1 shallow dish.
Storage: Fridge for 24 hours or freeze.
Servings: 8 sausages.

- Drain the beans well and place in the blender with the raisins, cumin, peanut butter, tomato purée and oats.
- Coarsely grate the carrot and add to the mixture.
- Process until no whole beans can be seen but the mixture is still coarse.
- Beat the egg in a bowl and put the breadcrumbs into a shallow dish.
- Divide the bean mixture into eight. The mixture should be fairly firm – if not, put a little flour on your hands.

- Take each of the eight portions and shape into a sausage. Dip the sausage in the egg and then in the breadcrumbs.
- Heat the oil in the frying pan and cook the sausages for about 5 minutes, until they are heated through and nicely browned.

Tips

- You can make these with any beans, including cannellini, borlotti, haricot and black-eyed beans.

Mushroom loaf

This recipe contains two powerful antioxidants as it combines selenium-rich mushrooms with tomato purée, just about the best source of lycopene around.

2 tsp olive oil
1 onion
175g mushrooms
75g tomato purée
100g granary bread
½ tsp yeast extract (such as Marmite)
30g Cheddar cheese, grated
extra oil for greasing

Preparation time: 20 minutes plus 20 minutes cooking.
Equipment: 1 frying pan, 1 loaf tin and 1 food processor.
Storage: Fridge for 1–2 days or freeze.
Servings: Makes a small loaf, enough for 2 adults and 1 baby for lunch, or slice and put in the freezer for several lunches or snacks.

- Preheat the oven to 200°C/400°F/gas mark 6.
- Grease the loaf tin and line with greaseproof paper or baking parchment.
- Dice the onion. Heat the oil in the frying pan and fry the onion for 1–2 minutes.
- Chop the mushrooms into small pieces, no more than 1cm cubes, and fry with the onion until soft.
- Meanwhile, make your bread into breadcrumbs using the food processor.
- Add the breadcrumbs, tomato purée, yeast extract and grated cheese to the pan and combine all the ingredients well.
- Transfer the mixture to the loaf tin and press down well.

- Bake for 20 minutes then leave to cool in the tin for 5–10 minutes before turning out.

Tips

- Instead of making this as one loaf you can make individual portions by using a muffin tin.

Japanese tofu patties

These are inspired by a Japanese dish called ganmodoki. Tofu is a good source of protein and calcium, but some babies find it a little rubbery in stir-fries – here the texture's not too dissimilar to an omelette or pancake.

½ red pepper
3 spring onions
1 carrot
1 garlic clove, crushed
2½cm fresh ginger, grated
¼ tsp ground coriander
2 tsp rapeseed oil
2 tsp sesame oil (or more rapeseed oil)
350–400g block tofu
2 eggs

Preparation time: 30 minutes.
Equipment: 1 mixing bowl and 1 or 2 frying pans.
Storage: Fridge for 24 hours or freeze. Reheat under the grill or in the oven.
Servings: 12 patties, enough for 2 adults and 2 children.

- Dice the pepper. Cut the spring onions in half lengthways and finely slice them. Peel and grate the carrot.
- Heat one teaspoon of sesame oil and one of rapeseed oil and fry the vegetables with the coriander, ginger and garlic for 5 minutes, until soft.
- Meanwhile, drain the tofu and place in a mixing bowl, then mash roughly with a fork.
- Make a well in the centre of the tofu and add the eggs. Beat the eggs lightly, then combine with the tofu.
- Add the cooked vegetables to the tofu and eggs and mix.
- Heat the rest of the oil in the frying pan and spoon in one heaped tablespoonful of mixture for each patty. You should be able to make six at a time.

- Cook for about 5 minutes on each side, until browned.

Tips

- These make a good family meal with a few stir-fried vegetables and some rice or noodles.
- Extras make an easy lunch with leftover pasta, potatoes or pitta.

Rice with butternut squash and chickpeas

A simple but tasty all-in-one meal that the whole family can enjoy together.

2 tsp olive oil
1 onion
½ red pepper
1 garlic clove, crushed
1 butternut squash
1 × 400g tin chickpeas
½ tsp sweet paprika
a few fresh sage leaves
150g basmati rice
1 low salt stock cube made up with 500ml boiling water

Preparation time: 25 minutes plus 15 minutes simmering.
Equipment: 1 deep-sided frying pan with lid.
Storage: Fridge for 1–2 days or freeze.
Servings: 2 adults and 1 baby.

- Chop the onion and pepper into 1cm cubes.
- Cut the butternut squash in half, scoop out the seeds and discard, remove the skin and cut into 1cm cubes.
- Heat the oil in the pan, then add the onion, pepper, butternut squash and crushed garlic and cook for about 10 minutes over a medium heat, until the squash is beginning to brown.
- Chop the sage and add to the pan along with the paprika, rice and chickpeas. Stir for 1 minute.
- Add the stock, stir and bring to the boil. Cover with a lid and leave to simmer for 10–15 minutes until the liquid has been absorbed and the rice and squash both look ready.

Tips

- You can squash the chickpeas for your baby to avoid choking if she hasn't had them before.
- This tastes delicious with a little feta cheese crumbled on top, but this is too salty for babies so grate some Cheddar on your baby's portion instead.
- If you want to spice it up a bit, you can add a little cinnamon, cumin and turmeric instead of the sage and paprika.

Broccoli pesto

Pesto is a favourite with many babies and children, and with parents because it's so handy. This version has the added benefit of broccoli, which is rich in vitamin C as well as lutein, which is a potent antioxidant and is important for eye health.

1 small broccoli (about 200g)
100ml water
20g pine nuts
handful fresh basil
1 garlic clove
20g pecorino, parmesan or other cheese, grated
2 tsp olive oil
spaghetti

Preparation time: 15–20 minutes.
Equipment: 1 saucepan and 1 food processor.
Storage: Fridge for 1–2 days or freeze.
Servings: 2 adults and 1 baby.

- Prepare the spaghetti according to the instructions on the packet.
- Cut the broccoli into small florets. Place them in the pan with the water, bring to the boil and simmer for about 3 minutes, until just cooked.
- Place the pine nuts on a piece of foil and toast under the grill until slightly browned. Keep a close eye as it doesn't take long.
- Put the pine nuts and garlic in a food processor and whizz to produce a coarse paste.
- Put the drained broccoli in the food processor, along with the basil, grated cheese and olive oil. Keep any cooking water and add to the pesto as needed.
- Purée the whole mixture until smooth and mix with the cooked spaghetti.

Tips

- Serve with a little more cheese grated on top. It is better to add Cheddar to your baby's portion as it contains less than half the amount of salt found in pecorino.

> 66 I made the broccoli pesto with Cheddar and found it worked well too. My little one is usually suspicious of anything green but this was a success. 99
> Christine, mum to Luca, 3 years, and Theo, 3 months

Pasta with creamy tomato and butter bean sauce

A quick but satisfying midweek dinner. Butter beans are great for babies as they are larger and softer than many other beans and have a slightly creamy texture.

1 tbsp rapeseed oil
1 onion
2 cloves garlic, crushed
150g carrots
1 × 400g tin chopped tomatoes
1 × 400g tin butter beans
2 tbsp tomato purée
1 tsp dried basil, or use fresh basil
½ tsp dried parsley, or use fresh parsley
¼ tsp sugar
1 tbsp cream cheese (optional)
pasta

Preparation time: 10 minutes plus 10–15 minutes cooking.
Equipment: 1 deep-sided frying pan and 1 saucepan.
Storage: Fridge for 24 hours or freeze.
Servings: 2 adults and 1 baby.

- Cook the pasta according to the instructions on the packet.
- Dice the onion. Heat the oil in the pan and fry the onion along with the crushed garlic for a couple of minutes until soft.
- Peel the carrots and grate them coarsely into the pan. Cook for a few more minutes.

- Add the tomatoes, drained beans, tomato purée, basil, parsley and sugar. Mix and leave to simmer for 10–15 minutes. Add a little water if needed.
- Stir in the cream cheese and serve with the cooked pasta.

Tips

- Babies need a higher ratio of sauce to pasta than adults so that they don't fill up on pasta without getting all the nutrients that the sauce contains.
- Babies can eat this as it is, or have it mashed or chopped.

> 66 *Daisy hadn't tasted butter beans before, but they're a really useful finger food. Just the right size to pick up, so she could get on and eat this whole dish without any help from me.* 99
> **Emma, mum to Daisy, 11 months**

Tuna carbonara

This creamy tuna and mushroom sauce makes a nice change to tomatoey sauces and it contains much less salt and saturated fat than traditional carbonara made with bacon.

1 tbsp rapeseed oil
½ small onion
2 cloves garlic, crushed
4 mushrooms
1 tbsp plain flour
250ml milk
1 × 160g tin tuna in spring water
20g parmesan cheese or similar hard cheese, grated
2 tbsp fresh basil
spaghetti or tagliatelle

Preparation time: 25 minutes.
Equipment: 1 deep-sided frying pan and 1 saucepan.
Storage: Fridge for 24 hours or freeze.
Servings: 2 adults and 1 baby.

- Cook the spaghetti or tagliatelle according to the instructions on the packet.
- Dice the onion. Heat the oil in the pan and fry the onion along with the crushed garlic for a couple of minutes until soft.

- Chop the mushrooms and add them to the pan. Fry for a few minutes longer.
- Add the flour to the pan and mix well so that it coats the vegetables.
- Add the milk and bring to the boil, stirring all the time.
- Drain the tuna, then mix it into the sauce, along with the grated cheese.
- Chop the basil and stir it into the sauce.
- Drain the pasta, mix with the sauce and serve.

Tips

- Serve with peas or steamed broccoli on the side.
- Mash or chop your baby's portion or serve it as it is.

66 *Emilia wolfed this down. Once she'd had enough off the spoon, I put some on her tray and she scooped it up with her fingers and ate it that way. My increasingly fussy 3-year-old also ate a plateful, so a definite thumbs up!* 99
Laura, mum to Sofia, 3 years, and Emilia, 9 months

Salmon and oat patties

Just like fish cakes, but made with oats instead of potatoes. For babies this means they don't fall apart so easily and for you it means no need for peeling, boiling and mashing potatoes.

2 salmon fillets or steaks (about 300g)
½ small onion
80–100g oats
1 tbsp lemon juice
½ level tsp Dijon mustard
2 eggs
1 tbsp rapeseed oil

Preparation time: 20 minutes.
Equipment: 1 frying pan and 1 mixing bowl.
Storage: Fridge for 1–2 days or freeze.
Servings: 2 adults and 1 baby – approximately 10 patties.

- Put the salmon in a microwave-safe bowl, cover with cling film, pierce the cling film with a fork and put the bowl in the microwave for about 2 minutes until the salmon is just cooked.

- Remove the skin from the salmon and flake the fish with a fork, removing any bones you find.
- Dice the onion very finely and add to the bowl, along with 80g of oats, the lemon juice, mustard and eggs. Mix well. Add extra oats, up to 20g more, if needed to make the mixture firm enough to handle.
- Using your hands, form the mixture into balls a little larger than a ping-pong ball. Flatten the balls gently with your hands so that they are no more than 1cm thick and put them on a plate.
- Heat the oil in a frying pan and fry the patties for about 3–4 minutes on each side until nicely browned.

Tips

- Serve with stir-fried vegetables, mushy peas (see p141) or a mixed salad.
- Adults might enjoy these with some horseradish sauce mixed with mayonnaise.

> 66 *Reuben declared these were very yummy and my partner and I definitely agreed. Sam was able to hold them well and enjoyed them as finger food. They definitely held together better than fish cakes and will be a regular fixture on our family menu from now on.* 99
> **Sarah, mum to Reuben, 4 years, and Sam, 9 months**

Moroccan sardine balls in tomato sauce

This is a milder version of a traditional dish, which you can spice up if you wish. You can prepare the sardine balls earlier in the day, then make the sauce when you're ready to eat.

For the sardine balls:
100g rice (any type)
2 × 120g tins sardines in oil or brine
1 garlic clove, crushed
1 tsp lemon juice
¼ tsp ground cumin
¼ tsp sweet paprika

For the tomato sauce:
2 tsp olive oil
½ yellow pepper
1 garlic clove, crushed

> 1 bay leaf
> ¼ tsp cumin
> ¼ tsp sweet paprika
> 500g passata

Preparation time: 30 minutes plus 15 minutes simmering.
Equipment: 1 saucepan, 1 frying pan, 1 bowl and 1 hand-held blender.
Storage: Fridge for 24 hours or freeze.
Servings: 14 sardine balls – enough for 2 adults and 1 baby.

- Cook the rice with about 300ml of water or according to the instructions on the packet.
- Drain the sardines well, rinse in cold water to remove most of the salt and place in a bowl (including the skin and bones).
- Using a hand-held blender, purée the sardines so that they form a smooth paste.
- Mix in the crushed garlic, lemon juice, cumin and paprika.
- When the rice is cooked, mix it thoroughly with the fish mixture using a fork.
- Take walnut-sized pieces of the mixture and form them into balls. These can be put in the fridge until you are ready to use them.
- To make the sauce, cut the pepper into thin strips.
- Heat the olive oil in the frying pan and cook the pepper with the crushed garlic for 3–4 minutes until soft.
- Add the remaining ingredients and cook for another 5 minutes.
- Add the sardine balls to the pan, spoon over some of the sauce and cook for 10–15 minutes, turning occasionally, until cooked through.

Tips

- This dish can be eaten as it is, or you can have it with some couscous, depending on appetites.
- Traditionally this would be made with fresh sardines but it can be difficult to remove the bones. The bones in tinned sardines are very soft, easy to purée and very rich in calcium. If you're not keen on sardines, you can try making it with salmon instead.
- Some babies may prefer the sardine balls broken up and mixed with the sauce.

Egg fried rice

This is a good way to use up leftover rice and it can be adapted to use up whatever vegetables you have in the fridge or freezer.

> 1 tbsp rapeseed or sesame oil
> 4 spring onions
> ½ red pepper
> 150g frozen soya beans or peas
> 300g cooked rice
> 125g cooked chicken or prawns
> 2 eggs

Preparation time: 15–20 minutes.
Equipment: 1 frying pan.
Storage: Eat straight away as the rice and chicken are being reheated here, so can't be reheated again.
Servings: 2 adults and 1 baby.

- Thinly slice the spring onions and dice the red pepper.
- Heat the oil in the frying pan and fry the spring onions and pepper for 5 minutes until soft. Add the rice, chicken or prawns and beans or peas. Stir well, breaking up any lumps of rice, for 3–4 minutes until hot.
- Beat the eggs together in a cup.
- Push the rice mixture to the edges of the pan and pour the egg mixture into the space in the centre.
- Stir the egg until lightly scrambled, then combine with the rest of the mixture and make sure it's all heated through.

Tips

- If you have just a little leftover rice you can make a single portion for your baby. You can make a vegetarian version without chicken or prawns if you like – maybe fry up a little mushroom or use any leftover veg you have, such as carrot or broccoli.
- Leftover rice is safe to use as long as it has been cooled and placed in the fridge straightaway, and kept for no more than one day. Do not re-use rice that has been left standing at room temperature for an hour or more, as this can cause bacteria to grow.

Sage and onion sausages

Sausages are notoriously unhealthy and packed with saturated fat and salt. These are much healthier and still make a comforting supper with mashed potato, cabbage and gravy.

½ onion
6 sage leaves
250g lean minced pork
40g wholemeal breadcrumbs (1 slice bread)
2 tbsp olive oil
2 tbsp plain flour

Preparation time: 20 minutes plus 10–15 minutes cooking.
Equipment: 1 frying pan and 1 mixing bowl.
Storage: Fridge for 24 hours or freeze.
Servings: 10 sausages – enough for 2 adults and 2 children.

- Peel and finely dice the onion.
- Heat one tablespoon of oil in the frying pan and fry the onion for 2–3 minutes until soft.
- Finely chop the sage leaves and prepare the breadcrumbs if not already done.
- Put the fried onion, sage, breadcrumbs and pork together in the mixing bowl and combine well using a fork.
- Put the flour on one side of a dinner plate and lightly flour your hands. Take a spoonful of the mixture and form it into a sausage shape. Roll it lightly in the flour and put it on the edge of the plate. Repeat until you have 10 sausages.
- Heat one tablespoon of oil in the frying pan and fry the sausages for 10–15 minutes until browned on the outside and cooked through.

Tips

- If you want to make the mixture smoother you can mix the ingredients in a food processor rather than just using a fork.
- These go well with homemade ketchup (p183).

> 66 *Reuben loves sausages but I am reluctant to feed them to my family too often as they're so unhealthy, so these are a welcome alternative. They were very tasty and proved a great finger food option for baby Sam.* 99
> **Sarah, mum to Reuben, 4 years, and Sam, 9 months**

Meatballs

This is an easy basic recipe, which you can adapt by adding different herbs, substituting pork for the beef (or using a mixture) or adding a handful of breadcrumbs.

500g lean minced beef
1 egg
1 small onion
1–2 tsp fresh herbs, finely chopped (e.g. rosemary, thyme)
1 tbsp tomato purée
1 tbsp rapeseed oil

Preparation time: 20 minutes plus 10 minutes cooking.
Equipment: 1 frying pan and 1 mixing bowl.
Storage: Fridge for 24 hours or freeze.
Servings: 20 meatballs – enough for 2 meals for 2 adults and 1 baby. Half of the uncooked meatballs can go in the freezer for another day.

- Very finely dice the onion and chop the herbs.
- Mix the mince, egg, onion, herbs and tomato purée in a large bowl and, using your hands, shape into about 20 walnut-sized meatballs.
- These can be placed in the fridge for later or cooked straight away.
- Heat the oil in a frying pan until sizzling and fry the meatballs for 8–10 minutes until nicely browned. Break one in half to check that there is no pinkness left.

Tips

- Serve with spaghetti or tagliatelle and basic tomato sauce (p38).
- To reheat the meatballs, place them on an oiled baking tray at 200°C/400°F/ gas mark 6 for 10–15 minutes.
- These can also be flattened into little patties or sausage shapes to make them easier for your baby to handle.

Minced lamb hotpot

This is a good warming meal and it doesn't take as long to cook as a regular hotpot with chunks of lamb.

> 4 medium potatoes
> 1 onion
> 1 carrot
> 1 leek
> 1 tbsp olive oil or rapeseed oil (plus an extra drizzle)
> 350g lean minced lamb
> 1 × 400g tin chopped tomatoes
> 2 bay leaves
> 4 sage leaves, chopped
> 1 tbsp fresh thyme, chopped
> 1 very low salt stock cube made up with 250ml water

Preparation time: 30 minutes plus 35 minutes cooking.
Equipment: 1 saucepan, 1 large frying pan and 1 casserole dish.
Storage: Fridge for 1–2 days or freeze.
Servings: 2 adults and 2 children or 15–20 baby portions.

- Preheat the oven to 160°C/320°F/gas mark 3.
- Bring a pan of water to the boil for cooking the potatoes.
- Peel the potatoes and chop them into 1cm thick slices. When the water is boiling put the slices into the pan and give it a stir to make sure they don't stick together. Bring it back to the boil and simmer for 5 minutes with the lid on.
- Meanwhile, peel and dice the onion and carrot. Chop the leek in half lengthways, give it an extra wash if needed, then slice it thinly.
- Heat the oil in the pan and sauté the onion and leek for 3–5 minutes.
- Push the vegetables to the sides of the pan and put the minced lamb in the space in the centre. Over a fairly high heat, brown the mince by breaking it up with a spoon or spatula and moving it around.
- Add the carrot, chopped tomatoes, herbs and stock. Bring to the boil and simmer for a few minutes until the carrot starts to soften.
- When the potatoes have simmered for 5 minutes, drain them and leave them to cool for a few minutes in the pan with the lid off.
- Transfer the lamb mixture to the casserole dish, then using a slotted spoon arrange the potato slices over the top. Start at the outside of the dish and go around the dish with overlapping slices before filling in the centre.
- Place the dish in the oven for 35 minutes, until browned on top. You may want to pop it under the grill for the last 5 minutes to brown it.

Tips

- Serve with cabbage, green beans or other vegetables.

Sweet potato gnocchi

Gnocchi are little Italian potato dumplings that can be eaten with sauces such as pesto or tomato sauce. They're a good alternative to pasta and the sweet potato provides extra vitamin C and beta-carotene.

> 1 sweet potato (about 200g before peeling)
> 1 potato (about 200g before peeling)
> 125g plain flour, plus extra for dusting
> 6 sage leaves
> 1 egg

Preparation time: 30 minutes plus 5 minutes cooking.
Equipment: 1 saucepan and 1 mixing bowl.
Storage: Best eaten straight away or fridge for 24 hours.
Servings: 2 adults and 1 baby.

- Prick the sweet and ordinary potatoes with a fork and place them in the microwave for about 10 minutes until soft.
- Finely chop the sage.
- When the potatoes are cooked, cut them in half, remove the skin and mash the flesh in a mixing bowl using a fork.
- Add the flour, sage and egg and mix well.
- Flour your hands, then scoop out the dough onto a floured work surface and form it into a rough patty shape.
- Divide the dough into quarters. Take one of these and roll it out into a 1cm thick sausage shape.
- Cut the sausage into 2½cm long pieces. You can leave these as they are, or smooth the ends of each piece and mark it with a fork.
- Bring a large pan of water to the boil. Gently add the gnocchi pieces and leave for a few minutes. When they are ready they will float to the top.
- When all the pieces are ready, remove them with a slotted spoon and serve.

Tips

- These are delicious served with basic tomato sauce (p38) and grated cheese, or with mackerel and tomato sauce (p86).

- Babies who are confident feeding themselves can have these as they are, but they can also be mashed slightly with the sauce to make them softer.

Potato farls

These are sometimes called potato bread or potato cakes and are popular in Northern Ireland, particularly with a fried breakfast. They're very easy to make and are a good way of using up leftover mashed potato.

2 potatoes (350g peeled weight) or similar amount of mashed potato
1 tbsp butter or margarine
100g self-raising flour, plus extra for dusting

Preparation time: 40 minutes.
Equipment: 1 saucepan and 1 griddle or large heavy frying pan.
Storage: Fridge for 1–2 days or freeze. Reheat under the grill.
Servings: 8 large or 16 small pieces – enough for 2 adults and 2 children.

- Peel the potatoes, cut them into cubes and place them in the pan. Cover the potatoes with water and bring to the boil. Simmer for about 10–15 minutes, until tender.
- Drain the potatoes and leave them in the pan for a few minutes to steam with the lid off.
- Mash the potatoes and stir in the flour and butter or margarine to form a dough.
- Divide the mixture in two. Take one of the pieces and roll it out on a floured work surface to form a circle about ½cm thick.
- Cut the circle into quarters, or into eight pieces if you want to make them smaller.
- Heat the frying pan. Throw in a little flour and when it browns (indicating the pan is hot enough) discard the flour and place the farls in the pan. Cook for 2–3 minutes on each side.
- While the first batch is cooking, roll out the other half of the dough and cut it into pieces.

Tips

- To bake the potato farls instead, heat a greased baking tray in the oven (200°C/400°F/gas mark 6), then place the farls on the hot tray and bake for 10–15 minutes, until browned.
- Instead of making triangular farls you can cut them into soldiers or use any pastry cutters you have.

Soft polenta

Polenta cooks in a few minutes and it is a good substitute for mashed potatoes when having stews or casseroles.

150g polenta
1 very low salt stock cube made up with 600ml water
25g Cheddar cheese, grated

Preparation time: 5 minutes.
Equipment: 1 saucepan.
Storage: Fridge for 1–2 days or freeze.
Servings: 2 adults and 1 baby.

- Bring the stock to the boil in a pan.
- Add the polenta in a slow, continuous stream while stirring with a wooden spoon.
- Bring it back to the boil and simmer for no more than a minute (the longer you cook it, the stiffer it gets).
- Take it off the heat and stir in the grated cheese.

Tips

- If you have any left over you can put it in the fridge and let it set, then slice it and brush with oil and fry or bake.
- Polenta has a fairly bland taste, to the adult palate at least, so it is best eaten with foods with a sauce.

Mushy peas

Peas are rich in thiamin, which is needed for the body to release energy from carbohydrates. They also supply vitamin C. Frozen peas are always a good standby but not all babies find them easy to eat so mushing them can work really well.

200g frozen peas
50ml water
2 mint leaves
1 tsp lemon juice
50g half-fat crème fraîche
salt and pepper to taste (for adults)

Preparation time: 10–15 minutes.
Equipment: 1 saucepan and 1 hand-held blender.
Storage: Fridge for 1–2 days or freeze.
Servings: 2 adults and 1 baby.

- Put the peas, water and mint leaves in the pan, bring to the boil and simmer for a few minutes.
- Add the crème fraîche and lemon juice to the pan and purée coarsely using the blender.

Tips

- This works well as a dip for babies too.
- Reduced-fat products are not recommended for babies as they need the extra calories provided by full-fat milk, yogurt and other dairy products. However, regular crème fraîche is nearly a third fat, which is more than anyone needs, so the half-fat version is used here.

Puddings and snacks

Fresh fruit and natural yogurt are still excellent puddings as your baby approaches 12 months, but there are a couple of recipes here, still involving fruit, that make a nice change. As your baby becomes more mobile and uses up energy rolling, crawling or pulling herself around, snacks become more important.

Raspberry clafoutis

This simple French country dessert is a cross between a cake and a baked custard. It is traditionally made with cherries, with the stones left in, but raspberries are a perfect substitute.

350g fresh or frozen raspberries
100g plain flour
2 tbsp caster sugar
3 eggs
200ml milk
½ tsp vanilla extract
1 tsp icing sugar
butter or margarine for greasing

Preparation time: 10 minutes plus 40 minutes cooking.
Equipment: 1 ovenproof dish, 1 mixing bowl and 1 hand-held blender.
Storage: Fridge for 1–2 days.
Servings: 6–8 adults and children.

- Preheat the oven to 180°C/350°F/gas mark 4.
- Grease the ovenproof dish and sprinkle over about a teaspoonful of flour.
- Mix the flour and sugar in a bowl, then whisk in the eggs, milk and vanilla extract using a hand-held blender until smooth and frothy.
- Place the raspberries in the bottom of the dish, pour the egg mixture over them and place in the oven for 30–40 minutes, until nicely browned.
- Remove from the oven and leave to cool slightly before sprinkling icing sugar over the top.

Tips

- The clafoutis is best eaten warm with a dollop of crème fraîche but is also nice cold.
- Don't worry if it seems to puff up when cooking and deflate while cooling – this is normal.
- Instead of making it with raspberries you can use strawberries, blueberries, apricots (fresh or tinned) or pears (peeled and sliced).

Cheats' cheesecake

This seems like a treat but takes only minutes to prepare and, unlike regular cheesecake, is low in fat and packed with vitamin C and other antioxidants.

150g mixed berries (fresh or frozen blueberries, raspberries, strawberries or other berries)
1 tsp cornflour
150g ricotta
10g soft brown sugar
couple of drops of vanilla essence
40g ginger biscuits (or digestives)

Preparation time: 15 minutes.
Equipment: 1 saucepan and 1 mixing bowl.
Storage: Fridge for 24 hours.
Servings: 2 adult and 1 baby portions

- Put the berries in a small pan and bring to the boil over a medium heat, stirring occasionally. No water is needed as the berries have a high water content.
- In a small cup mix the cornflour with 3 tsp of cold water until smooth. Add this to the berries and stir for a few minutes until the mixture thickens, then leave to cool.
- Put the biscuits in a food bag and break them up by rolling a rolling pin over the top, or with the back of a spoon.
- Mix together the ricotta, sugar and vanilla essence in a bowl.
- Assemble individual cheesecakes by spooning biscuit crumbs into the bottom of each dish, followed by the ricotta and then the fruit mixture.
- Place the dishes in the fridge to set.

Tips

- If you're short of time, you needn't cook the berries. They can be left as they are or just sliced or mushed.
- Try other fruit such as pineapple, mango or tinned blackcurrants or cherries.

66 *We've had this with berries and pears, and it's surprisingly nice made with bananas and a digestive base. I'm more used to the base of a cheesecake being solid but actually I think this way was easier for Elizabeth to manage.* 99
Emma, mum to Elizabeth, 14 months

Fruity oat cookies

These have no added sugar but you wouldn't guess it, as the dried fruit, cinnamon and vanilla make them taste delicious.

100g oats
50g wholemeal flour
½ tsp bicarbonate of soda
1 tsp cinnamon
50g sultanas
6 dried apricots
50ml rapeseed oil
100ml milk
1 egg
1 tsp vanilla essence

Preparation time: 15 minutes plus 15 minutes cooking.
Equipment: 1 mixing bowl, 1 measuring jug and 2 baking trays.
Storage: Airtight container for 3–4 days or freeze.
Servings: 20 cookies.

- Preheat the oven to 180°C/350°F/gas mark 4. Cover the baking trays with greaseproof paper.
- Put the oats, flour, bicarbonate of soda, cinnamon and sultanas into the mixing bowl.
- Chop the dried apricots and add them too. Give the mixture a stir.
- Measure the oil and milk into a measuring jug. Add the egg and vanilla and beat.
- Pour the wet ingredients into the mixing bowl and give everything a good stir.
- Place one teaspoon of mixture for each cookie onto the baking tray. You should get about 20 cookies. Use a fork or the back of a spoon to flatten the dollops slightly so that they're no more than 1cm thick.
- Place in the oven for 15 minutes.

Tips

- Feel free to replace the sultanas and apricots with other dried fruit. You can also add some chopped nuts or sesame seeds to the mixture.

Butternut squash and ginger cake

The butternut squash here provides vitamins A, C and E, while the treacle is a good source of potassium and iron – pretty good for a deliciously moist and spicy cake.

200g self-raising flour
1 tsp baking powder
1 tsp ground ginger
¼ tsp cinnamon
50g soft brown sugar
225g butternut squash
½ tsp fresh ginger, grated
100ml rapeseed oil
50g treacle
2 eggs (beaten)
2 tbsp milk (for a dairy-free version use apple or orange juice instead)
1 tbsp flaked almonds (optional)

Preparation time: 20 minutes plus 40 minutes cooking.
Equipment: 21cm diameter round cake tin, 1 mixing bowl and 1 hand-held blender (optional).
Storage: Airtight container for 2–3 days or freeze.
Servings: 10–15 slices (depending on size).

- Preheat the oven to 180°C/350°F/gas mark 4.
- Brush the cake tin with oil and line the bottom with greaseproof paper.
- Mix the flour, baking powder, ground ginger, cinnamon and sugar in a bowl.
- Peel and finely grate the butternut squash, or use a blender, and add the squash and ginger to the bowl.
- Make a well in the centre of the mixture and add the oil, eggs, treacle and milk.
- Stir the cake mixture so all the ingredients are well combined and put it into the prepared cake tin.
- Scatter the almond flakes over the top, if using, and bake for 40 minutes, until a skewer inserted in the centre comes out dry. If the top of the cake is becoming too brown, cover it loosely with foil until the centre is cooked.

> 66 *The kids loved the cake and so did everyone who had it. It wasn't too sweet, had a bit of a crunch on the outside but was moist inside. I cheated and bought cubed butternut squash, which I put straight in the blender to finely chop.* 99
> **Nancy, mum to Florence, 4 years, and Dylan, 17 months**

Hot milk buns

These are just like fruit buns but made with milk instead of water and without the sugar and salt that is usually included. As they take a while to make, it's good to do a large batch and put some in the freezer.

500g plain flour
1 sachet fast-acting dried yeast (7g)
100g dried mixed fruit
1 tsp mixed spice (optional)
50ml rapeseed oil
325ml milk
extra flour for dusting

Preparation time: 1 hour 40 minutes: 20 minutes preparation, 45 minutes rising, 25 minutes preparation, 10 minutes cooking.
Equipment: 2–3 baking trays and 2 mixing bowls.
Storage: Airtight container for 24 hours or freeze.
Servings: Makes 20 medium-sized buns or 40 small ones.

- Put the milk in the microwave for 2–3 minutes or heat it in a pan until it is warm but not boiling.
- Mix the flour, mixed spice, yeast, dried fruit and oil, then add the warm milk and mix to a soft dough.
- Turn the dough out onto a floured work surface and knead for 10 minutes. (Stretch a handful of the dough away from you, then fold it back over and push it into the centre. Turn the whole lump of dough a quarter circle and keep repeating.)
- Take a clean mixing bowl and brush the inside with oil, then place the dough in it and cover the bowl with cling film. Put it in a warm place until the dough has doubled in size, about 45 minutes.
- Preheat the oven to 200°C/400°F/gas mark 6. Brush two or three baking trays with oil.
- Turn the dough out onto a floured work surface and give it a quick knead. Divide the dough in half and then in half again. Keep going until you have 20 or 40 pieces. Using your hands, roll each piece into a sausage shape, or a ball if you prefer.
- Place the buns on a baking tray and bake for 10 minutes until browned on top. If you tap one it should sound hollow.
- Once cooked, leave the buns to cool on a wire rack.

Tips

- If you want to give the buns a shiny glaze, mix a heaped tablespoon of icing sugar with one tablespoon of water and brush the mixture over the buns while they are still warm.
- For a real treat, wait until the buns have cooled, then put white sugar icing on top, made with icing sugar and a drop of water.

Sweet potato and raisin muffins

These are made with very little sugar but have a lovely sweet taste, a bit like bread pudding but not as dense. They are the ultimate snack for slow release energy as they are made with three of the best low GI carbs: oats, wholemeal flour and sweet potatoes.

> 225g cooked sweet potato (or pop 1 large sweet potato in the microwave)
> 100g oats
> 250g plain yogurt
> 100g wholemeal flour
> 2 tsp baking powder
> ½ tsp mixed spice
> 1 tsp cinnamon
> 50g dark brown sugar (muscovado)
> 50g raisins
> 50ml rapeseed oil
> 1 egg
> 1 tsp vanilla essence

Preparation time: 25 minutes plus 15 minutes cooking.
Equipment: 2 muffin tins (9 per tray), 1 mixing bowl and 1 smaller bowl.
Storage: Airtight container for 1–2 days or freeze.
Servings: 18 muffins.

- Preheat the oven to 200°C/400°F/gas mark 6. Put paper cases in the muffin tins.
- Mix the oats and yogurt together in the smaller bowl and leave to stand.
- Place the flour, baking powder, spices, sugar and raisins in the mixing bowl.
- Beat together the oil, egg and vanilla essence. This can be done in a measuring jug.
- Add the sweet potato, oat mixture and oil mixture to the mixing bowl and stir well using a fork.
- Spoon the mixture into the muffin cases and bake for 15 minutes.

Tips

- If you like, you can add more spices and also try nutmeg and ginger.
- The raisins can be replaced with other dried fruit and you can also add walnuts or pecans to the mixture.

> 66 *These moist little treats are really quite deliciously moreish. I felt they were wholesome enough to serve Reuben for breakfast and to give to baby Sam (who I hadn't given anything to with added sugar previously!).* 99
> **Sarah, mum to Reuben, 4 years, and Sam, 9 months**

First birthday carrot cake

This carrot cake has more carrot and less sugar than other recipes, but it still tastes like a sweet treat, especially if you cover it in creamy icing. It's very easy to make, even if you've never baked a cake before, and the result is sure to impress guests both big and small.

225g self-raising flour (or gluten-free self-raising flour)
½ tsp baking powder
1 tsp cinnamon
½ tsp mixed spice
100g soft brown sugar
150g sultanas
225g carrot (peeled weight)
150ml rapeseed oil
2 eggs
For the icing:
25g margarine or butter
60g cream cheese
150g icing sugar

Preparation time: 20 minutes plus 30 minutes cooking.
Equipment: 21cm round cake tin and 1 mixing bowl.
Storage: Airtight container for 2–3 days or freeze.
Servings: 16 adults or 30 children.

- Preheat the oven to 180°C/350°F/gas mark 4. Grease the cake tin and line it with greaseproof paper.
- Place the flour, baking powder, cinnamon, mixed spice, sugar and sultanas in the mixing bowl. Stir the ingredients.
- Grate the carrot into the bowl and mix.
- Beat the oil and eggs together with a fork in a cup or jug. Add it to the mixing bowl and give everything a good stir.
- Put the mixture into the cake tin and bake for 30 minutes or until a skewer inserted in the centre comes out dry.

To make the icing:

- Cream together the margarine or butter and cream cheese.
- Mix in about half the icing sugar and then add the rest and beat with a spoon until smooth. Add a little extra icing sugar if it seems too runny.

- Spoon the icing over the top of the cake and spread it out with the back of the spoon.

Tips

- This recipe is nut-free as this is usually safest for a birthday party, but you can add 100g chopped walnuts to the mixture if you like.
- The cake tastes good without icing too – this would obviously reduce the sugar content for days when you're not celebrating a special occasion.
- To make an even healthier version without any added sugar, you can replace the soft brown sugar in the recipe with two large mashed bananas. You can also use wholemeal flour instead of white.

Snack ideas

- Bananas
- Breadsticks
- Rice cakes
- Mini pots of chopped fruit, such as grapes, kiwi or peach
- Dried fruit, for example raisins or chopped apricots
- Cheese and tomato scone biscuits (p100) and similar savoury snack recipes
- Ginger biscuits (p188), fruit and nut cereal bars (p189) and other sweet snack recipes

Meal plan for a 10- to 12-month-old baby

The five-day meal plan below shows how 10- to 12-month-old babies can meet all their nutrient requirements. In addition to the foods shown, babies should have three or four breastfeeds or 500–600ml of infant formula and also a cup of water with each meal and snack. Just like the previous meal plans, this one mainly includes family meals and very little bread or other convenience foods (p104). Compared with the meal plan for a 7- to 9-month-old, this one has more finger foods and dips, as babies this age are increasingly able and keen to feed themselves. The plan includes foods from previous sections as well as this one, so that babies eat an increasing range of foods.

Day	Breakfast	Snack	Lunch	Snack	Dinner
1	Weetabix with apricot and almond (p64)	Rice cakes	Leek and pea patty (p116), roast carrot and pepper with houmous Apple and mango purée (p51)	Raisins	Pasta with creamy tomato and butter bean sauce (p130) ½ a pear
2	Ready Brek with ½ a banana	Plum	Leftover pasta with avocado and yogurt dip (p43) and cherry tomatoes (halved) Kiwi fruit	Sweet potato and raisin muffin (p147)	Salmon and oat patty (p132) with avocado and yogurt dip (p43) and carrot sticks
3	Weetabix with sultanas and chopped walnuts	½ a banana	Minced lamb hotpot (p137) with broccoli Jar of baby pudding	Rice cakes with almond butter	Wrap (p70) with beany dip (p120) and leftover broccoli Cheats' cheesecake (p143)
4	Baby muesli Strawberries	Breadsticks	Wrap with salmon pâté (p67) with cucumber and tomato Apple and pear	Plum	Roast chicken, new potato, cauliflower, carrot and peas Raspberry clafoutis (p142)

Continued over page

Continued from overleaf

Day	Breakfast	Snack	Lunch	Snack	Dinner
5	Oaty pancake (p112) Apple, apricot and banana (p53)	Oaty pancake	Pitta and leftover cauliflower and carrot with houmous Raspberry clafoutis (p142)	Breadstick and cubes of cheese	Rice with butternut squash and chickpeas (p128) Strawberries

This meal plan meets the requirements for energy, protein, potassium, calcium, magnesium, phosphorus, iron, copper, zinc, chloride, selenium, iodine, thiamin, riboflavin, niacin, folic acid and vitamins A, B6, B12, C, D and E. It also contains less than 1g of salt per day, which is the maximum babies should have.

Dos, don'ts and FAQs for your 10- to 12-month-old

Do

- Give your baby plenty of iron-rich foods such as fortified breakfast cereals, meat, fish, beans, lentils and dried fruit.
- Introduce new flavours such as beetroot, ginger, coriander and mild curry.
- Encourage your baby to feed herself with a spoon and her fingers.
- Keep offering foods even if your baby doesn't eat them. The more times you offer them, the more likely it is she'll eat them.
- Give foods (especially vegetables) individually as well as in mixed dishes so that your baby gets used to the different flavours and textures.

Don't

- Let your baby fill up on milk, juice or snacks between meals.
- Regularly spoon-feed your baby. She needs to learn to feed herself with a spoon, fork or her fingers.
- Clean your baby while she's eating. Wait until she's finished.

- Encourage playing with food by laughing or joining in.
- Purée your baby's meals. Chopping is fine but the blender is needed only for soups and dips now.
- Give your baby low-fat dairy foods such as yogurt and cheese. She needs the nutrients found in full-fat varieties.

FAQs

Q: What finger foods can I pack for eating out?

A: Sandwiches are an obvious choice and there are lots of suggestions for healthy fillings on page 164. Cooked vegetables such as green beans and carrot can also be eaten out but softer ones such as butternut squash can be much more messy. Other good finger foods for eating out include pieces of cold omelette (p81), baked courgette fingers (p73) or leek and pea patties (p116). For pudding, try banana or dried fruit, or raw apple if your baby can handle it. Pouches of fruit purée are another option. Finally, don't forget a good bib, preferably one with a pocket or pouch for catching the bits, and plenty of wipes.

Q: My baby screams when I put her in her high chair. Should I just ignore it?

A: If your daughter's having fun exploring the world, then meals can be seen as a bit of an inconvenience, so try to make them as pleasurable as possible. Put something on the table or tray that you know she likes, such as a few raisins or pieces of rice cake, just to get her in. Maybe for a few days make her favourite meals so that you're only tackling the high chair problem rather than having to deal with issues relating to food as well. Then sit down with her and make it a sociable occasion. And as soon as she looks like she's had enough, remember that means the meal is finished, so don't try to get another few mouthfuls in – just get her out of the chair and move on.

Meals should be at regular times and snacks should be healthy and not too big, then she'll be more ready to eat. You could also try putting her bib on before she gets in the high chair, to ease the transition. If she doesn't eat a meal in her chair, don't follow her round offering her bits of food, as this just teaches her that there's an alternative to being strapped in a high chair. With older children you can insist that they stay at the table for a certain amount of time, but it's important that it's always the baby's or child's decision whether or not she eats. The choice isn't between eating or playing – they need to be at the table and then they can decide to eat or not eat.

Q: My baby hates anything green. What can I do?

A: If your baby refuses certain foods, the most important thing to remember is not to make a fuss or try to force or even cajole her into eating them. Babies soon learn that refusing broccoli results in mum putting on a great song and dance act or dad playing airplanes, which is all great fun. Instead, take a three-pronged attack: try alternatives, present the food in different ways and keep trying. This strategy is the same for any food that a baby or child is refusing to eat.

When it comes to alternatives, there are lots of green vegetables to try: broccoli, spinach, cabbage, sprouts, kale, spring greens and even cauliflower (not green but similar nutritionally). Offer plenty of other vegetables too, such as carrots, tomatoes, peppers and squash. Next, there are plenty of different ways for presenting green vegetables: boiled, steamed, in stir-fries, broccoli pesto (p129), bubble and squeak cakes (p92) or leek and pea patties (p116). You can also disguise the flavour in a mixed purée or tomato-based pasta sauce, but this isn't a long-term solution. You want your baby to enjoy greens without any 'tricks', so it's vital to keep trying. If you stop giving your baby broccoli, you can't blame her for not eating it. It's estimated that children need to be offered foods between five and 20 times on average before they accept them. Also try greens when your baby is hungry, maybe before other foods and when you're eating them too.

Q: How long should meals take?

A: This is hard to say as babies vary enormously in the speed at which they eat, how much time they need for 'exploring' their food and how restless they are. Some may take just 10 minutes and others 40 minutes, with 20 minutes probably about average. Sharing meals is beneficial for both slow and fast eaters as it encourages those who want to get down to stay engaged and sit at the table, and it helps those who are slow or easily distracted to get on with their meal.

If your baby is itching to get out of the high chair after 5 minutes and a couple of mouthfuls, it's good to encourage her to stay longer, even if she doesn't eat anything more. What you don't want is for her to get down hungry and then want milk or something else instead, or for you to worry she hasn't eaten very much and offer snacks. It's good for babies to get used to the idea that there are times to eat and times to do other things and not think about food. If meals regularly take more than half an hour, it's worth thinking about the tactics for tackling slow eating on p108.

Q: How can I stop my baby playing with food and making such a mess?

A: Playing with food is a baby's way of familiarising themselves with it and an important part of accepting and enjoying it, so it's not something you should try to stop altogether. However, it can be a sign that your baby has had enough to eat. If this is the case, it's probably best to get her out of her high chair when she stops eating and is just playing. Also, try not to laugh as your baby empties a bowl of pasta and sauce over the high chair tray and enthusiastically spreads it out. If spoons or other things are thrown or dropped, don't keep returning them like a well-trained dog.

You can also try to minimise the amount of cleaning required by choosing a bib carefully. A long one with sleeves may be best. And you could get a splash mat to cover the floor. If there are certain times of the day when you really can't cope with the mess, then choose less messy foods for that meal, for example the types of foods your baby could eat when you're out (p153). Then your baby can have messier meals, such as spaghetti, soup or dips, in the evening when you can take her straight from the table to the bath.

Don't be tempted to wipe her face or clean up while she's still eating as this could put her off and make mealtimes stressful. As your baby's dining skills improve she'll naturally become a tidier eater, so there's some comfort in knowing that it's not going to be this messy for long.

5 Feeding your toddler and beyond

As your baby reaches her first birthday she'll become increasingly independent in her eating habits and in other aspects of life. Toddlers can have strong feelings about what they want to eat and how they want to do it. The key is to avoid food battles and allow your toddler to eat what she wants, but only from the healthy foods that are available to her. Your job is to provide regular nutritious meals and snacks, and then give your toddler plenty of control. Growth slows down considerably in the second year of life, so a slump in appetite is quite normal and there's no need to encourage your toddler to eat more.

All the recipes in this section are for dishes that adults will enjoy as much as toddlers. As children get older it becomes even more important to eat together. Research shows that children who share in family meals have healthier diets, a higher fruit and vegetable intake and are more willing to eat new foods.

Of course, family meals may not be easy to achieve. Many parents get used to putting their baby to bed at about 7.30p.m. then having a relaxed dinner. But even if this is the case, it should still be possible to share breakfast and lunch. If you've tried the odd shared meal and not found it very relaxing, don't be put off. The more often you eat together, the easier and more enjoyable it gets.

Daily requirements for a toddler

Each day, try to offer your toddler:

- 3–4 servings of starchy foods (e.g. bread, pasta, potatoes)
- 4–5 servings of fruit and vegetables (different colours if possible)
- 2 servings of meat, fish, eggs, tofu, lentils or other pulses
- 300–350ml of milk or about two servings of yogurt or cheese – if your toddler is generally eating well, you can give cows' milk as her main drink.

Breakfasts

Breakfast is an important meal for busy toddlers and helps set them up for the morning. Starting the day well avoids the need for biscuits or other snacks as soon as you go out or arrive at a playgroup, which can lead to a cycle of being too full for lunch and then wanting more snacks in the afternoon.

The breakfast suggestions on page 67 are still good choices at this age. As your baby gets older you may think about moving on to 'kids' cereals', but it's generally better to steer clear of this section of the supermarket. Most of the products there are highly refined and have lots of added sugar, and some have a fair amount of salt too. Foods for babies are highly regulated, but not those marketed for children. There are some reasonable cereals available, but you need to read the labels to identify them.

Choosing a breakfast cereal

Unhealthy choices
It's best to avoid any cereal that mentions:

- honey
- chocolate
- frosted
- syrup.

If you look at the small print, they're generally 25% to 35% sugar.

Healthy choices

Instead look for:

- wholegrain or wholewheat
- added vitamins and iron
- less than 5g sugar per 100g.

Healthy cereals include Weetabix, Oatibix, Ready Brek and own brand versions of these, but not the flavoured varieties.

Compromise choices

If toddlers won't eat any of the 'healthy choices', look for:

- wholegrain or wholewheat
- added vitamins and iron
- less than 20g sugar per 100g.

These include Shreddies, multigrain shapes and own brand versions of these, but again not the frosted or flavoured varieties.

Homemade muesli

This takes minutes to make and is packed with nutrients toddlers often miss out on, including iron from the dried apricots and sultanas, and selenium from the Brazil nuts. The basic recipe can be adapted to make a nut-free or wheat-free version.

125g porridge oats (not jumbo oats, which can be a chore to chew)
2 Weetabix (or other brands of wheat bisks)
1 tbsp sultanas
5 dried apricots
6 Brazil nuts
10 almonds

Preparation time: 10 minutes.
Equipment: 1 airtight container.
Storage: Airtight container for several weeks.
Servings: Enough for 4 adult and 2 toddler portions or 8–10 toddler portions.

- Weigh the oats and sultanas into your container and crumble in the Weetabix.

- Put the nuts on a chopping board and chop finely, then chop the apricots too.
- Mix everything together.

Tips

- Weetabix-type cereal is used here because it contains less salt and sugar and more iron than most high-fibre wheat cereals. Remember: organic varieties aren't fortified with iron so contain much less than regular versions.
- Finely chopping the nuts means the nutrients they contain can be digested more easily, rather than passing straight through.
- To make a nut-free version simply leave out the nuts and add a variety of different dried fruits instead. Or, to make it wheat-free, use Oatibix or puffed rice instead of Weetabix.
- Choose dried apricots rather than 'ready to eat', which are partially rehydrated and need to be kept in the fridge once opened.

66 *Rufus loved making this, including his own label! He has a nut allergy so we added sultanas, dates, apricots and cranberries. He was so excited to eat it, and really enjoyed it. He particularly liked looking for the 'hiding fruit'! A massive success!* 99
Ellie, mum to Rufus, 2½ years

Blueberry breakfast cake

Yes 'let them eat cake!', even for breakfast – providing it's packed with nutrient-rich foods such as oats, eggs, milk and blueberries.

200g blueberries, fresh or frozen
100g oats
150g plain flour
50g wholemeal flour
2 tbsp demerara sugar
2 tsp baking powder
175ml fromage frais or yogurt
100ml milk
2 eggs
2 tbsp cornflour
butter, margarine or oil for greasing

Preparation time: 15 minutes plus 30 minutes cooking.
Equipment: 23cm round cake tin or 20cm square tin and 1 mixing bowl.
Storage: Airtight container for 1–2 days or freeze.
Servings: About 12 toddler portions.

- Preheat the oven to 200°C/400°F/gas mark 6.
- Grease the cake tin and sprinkle with flour.
- Mix together the oats, both flours, sugar and baking powder.
- In a measuring jug or bowl, mix together the fromage frais or yogurt, milk, eggs and cornflour, and beat with a fork.
- Pour the egg mixture into the dry ingredients and mix well.
- Fold in the blueberries, then transfer the mixture to the cake tin and bake for 25–30 minutes, until it is nicely browned and a skewer inserted in the centre comes out dry.

Tips

- This is ideal for babies who have gone off their usual breakfast or those who need to eat on the go.
- Instead of blueberries, try making it with raspberries, pears or a mixture of sultanas and grated apple.
- To make a wheat-free version, replace the flour with gluten-free flour.

> 66 *This is quick, easy and ideal for BLW. Ivy had some for breakfast yesterday and on the go at snack time today and enjoyed it both times. As it's healthy, I don't mind giving in to her demands for 'more cake'!* 99
> **Adele, mum to Ivy, 19 months**

Lunches and dinners

As children get older they tend to eat different foods at lunchtime compared with the evening. There's no reason why they can't have lasagne or stir-fry at midday, but if they're eating with you or other children and you're having a sandwich or soup, they're now better able to join in so it makes sense for them to have the same or at least something fairly similar. It's very easy to end up in a rut and make cheese sandwiches every day because the ingredients are to hand and you know they'll be eaten, but do try to have a bit of variety. Having cheese on toast for a change doesn't count, by the way! Instead, find a few different lunches that work for you, hopefully one with fish and another with beans or lentils. And when you have sandwiches, try to have some vegetables or salad with them. Also, it's good to have something other than bread for lunch at least a couple of days a week, perhaps a baked potato, or salad made with leftover pasta.

Sardine pâté

Tins of sardines are a great standby in the cupboard and can be just mashed on a slice of toast. However, they have quite a strong flavour and aren't popular with everyone. This recipe is simple, doesn't taste as fishy as plain sardine, and goes well in sandwiches as well as on toast.

1 × 120g tin sardines in oil or brine
1 heaped tbsp cream cheese
1 tbsp tomato purée
1 tbsp chopped fresh parsley
black pepper

Preparation time: 5 minutes.
Equipment: 1 bowl.
Storage: Fridge for 24 hours.
Servings: 1 adult and 1 toddler.

- Drain the sardines, rinse to remove most of the salt and place in a bowl with the other ingredients.
- Mash well with a fork.

Tips

- This makes a very good sandwich with sliced tomato on granary bread.

Mushroom and watercress pâté

This simple pâté is packed with beta carotene, vitamin C, iron and a host of phytochemicals. It also tastes delicious.

1–2 tsp rapeseed or olive oil
1 onion
200g mushrooms (any kind)
50g watercress
100g cream cheese

Preparation time: 15 minutes.
Equipment: 1 deep-sided frying pan and 1 food processor or hand-held blender.
Storage: Fridge for 1–2 days or freeze.
Servings: 2 adults and 2 toddlers.

- Peel and dice the onion and finely slice the mushrooms.
- Heat the oil in the frying pan and fry the onion for 2 minutes, until soft but not brown.
- Add the mushrooms and fry for about 5 minutes until soft.
- Chop the watercress, add it to the pan and cook for a minute until wilted.
- Take the pan off the heat and stir in the cream cheese, then blend until smooth.

Tips

- Serve the pâté in pitta bread or on toast fingers, with some tomato and cucumber pieces.

66 *This is great, easy to make, and very popular with daddy! Rufus had it on bread fingers and said it was 'yummy yummy'!* 99
Ellie, mum to Rufus, 2 years

Tuna melt wraps

Toddlers seem to love wraps, and when they're sandwiched together with tuna and a little cheese they make a quick and nutritious lunch.

1 × 160g tin tuna in spring water
25g Cheddar or other cheese, grated
1 heaped tbsp cream cheese
2 soft wraps

Preparation time: 15 minutes.
Equipment: 1 small bowl and 1 plate.
Storage: Best eaten straight away but can be kept in the fridge for 24 hours.
Servings: 1 adult and 1 toddler.

- Preheat the grill to medium hot.
- Drain the tuna and mash it in the bowl using a fork.
- Add the cream cheese and grated Cheddar and mix well.

- Spread the mixture over one wrap and place it under the grill for 3–4 minutes.
- Press the other wrap down on top of the tuna mixture so you have a big sandwich and grill for 3–4 minutes more until browned.
- Turn the whole sandwich over and brown the other side.
- Cut it into wedges and serve.

Tips

- Eat the wrap with some chopped tomatoes, green beans or vegetable sticks.

Mushroom melt

Mushrooms smell great when they're cooking and this makes a good change from regular cheese on toast.

1 tsp olive oil
80g mushrooms
1 tbsp shallot or red onion, chopped finely
1 tbsp fresh parsley (optional)
30g Emmental or Gruyère cheese
3 slices granary bread
3 heaped tsp cream cheese

Preparation time: 10 minutes.
Equipment: 1 frying pan.
Storage: Best eaten straight away.
Servings: 1 adult and 1 toddler.

- Cut the mushrooms in half, then slice them.
- Heat the oil in the frying pan and fry the chopped onion or shallot and sliced mushrooms for 3–4 minutes until nicely browned, then take the pan off the heat.
- Meanwhile, put the bread in the toaster.
- Grate the cheese and chop the parsley if you're using it.
- When the toast is ready, spread each slice with cream cheese.
- Add the cheese and parsley to the pan and give everything a stir – the cheese will melt quickly. Then divide the mixture between the three slices of toast.

Salmon and apple toast topper

This takes just minutes to prepare and includes all the food groups in one go.

1 × 200g tin pink salmon
1 tbsp mayonnaise
1 apple
50g Jarlsberg, Leerdammer or Gruyère cheese, grated
black pepper
granary bread or rolls

Preparation time: 10 minutes.
Equipment: 1 bowl.
Storage: Fridge for 24 hours.
Servings: 2 adults and 1 toddler

- Drain the salmon and place it in a bowl. Remove the central bone, which looks like sections of spine, but leave the smaller bones for added calcium. You can leave the skin as well and just mash it with the fish using a fork.
- Stir in the mayonnaise, black pepper and the grated cheese.
- Peel and core the apple and grate it into the mixture.
- Lightly toast your bread or rolls, then spread the salmon mixture on top and place under the grill for about 5 minutes until it starts to brown.

Sandwich ideas

- Cream cheese and avocado
- Cheddar and tomato or cucumber
- Cheese and coleslaw
- Houmous and avocado
- Houmous and sweet pickle
- Houmous and grated carrot
- Peanut butter and grated carrot
- Butter bean and parsley pâté (p68)
- Mushroom and watercress pâté (p161)
- Soya bean and pea houmous (p69) in pitta
- Cream cheese and beetroot dip (p120) in pitta

- Egg mayonnaise
- Sliced hard-boiled egg with tomato
- Sliced omelette or tortilla (p82)
- Mashed sardine and hard-boiled egg
- Tuna with mayonnaise and sweetcorn or cucumber
- Sardine pâté (p161)
- Tinned salmon with cucumber
- Chicken and salad
- Roast beef and tomato

Toasted sandwiches and melts

- Pizza toast (tomato purée and Cheddar or mozzarella)
- Cheddar cheese and tomato toastie
- Grated cheese and grated apple on toast
- Mushroom melt (p163)
- Peanut butter, mashed sweet potato and a splash of orange juice
- Scrambled eggs (p45)
- Tuna melt wrap (p162)
- Mashed sardines (tinned in tomato sauce)
- Mashed sardines (tinned in oil) with lemon juice
- Sardine pâté (p161)
- Salmon pâté (p67)
- Salmon and apple toast topper (p164)

Trout pasta salad

This pasta salad makes a welcome change to sandwiches for lunch and is perfect for picnics away from home, as it contains all the food groups in one dish.

175g farfalle (pasta bows) or fusilli (twists) (uncooked weight)
2 trout fillets (or use salmon)
1 tsp lemon juice
8–10 baby sweetcorns (or 3 tbsp frozen or tinned sweetcorn)
10 cherry tomatoes

> *For the dressing:*
> 1 tbsp chopped fresh parsley
> 2 spring onions or a few chives
> 4 tbsp natural yogurt (or mashed avocado for a dairy-free version)
> 1–2 tsp cider vinegar or white wine vinegar
> 1 tsp olive or sesame oil
> ½ tsp Dijon mustard

Preparation time: 30 minutes.
Equipment: 2 saucepans (1 large, 1 small), 1 serving bowl and 1 baking tray.
Storage: Fridge for 24 hours.
Servings: 2 adults and 1 toddler.

- Cook the pasta in the large pan according to the instructions on the packet.
- Cook the baby sweetcorn in the small pan with ½–1cm of water or steam it for 4–5 minutes.
- Put the trout fillets on the baking tray, skin side up, and grill for 5 minutes. Turn them over, sprinkle with lemon juice, then grill for another 5 minutes, until cooked through but not dried out.
- Finely chop the spring onion (or chives) and parsley and mix them together in small bowl or cup along with all the other ingredients for the dressing.
- When the trout is cooked, flake the fish into the serving bowl, checking for bones and leaving behind the skin.
- When the pasta is cooked, drain it, then refill the pan with cold water and drain a couple more times. This will stop it from going mushy.
- Rinse the cooked sweetcorn in cold water too, then cut them lengthways and chop into small pieces (or bigger if that suits your baby better).
- Cut the cherry tomatoes in half.
- Add the pasta, sweetcorn, tomatoes and dressing to the serving bowl and mix everything together.

> 66 *The whole family enjoyed this and I will definitely be adding it to my repertoire. I didn't realise it was so easy to cook fish.* 99
> **Lorelei, mum to Blodwen, 4 years, and Annie, 2 years**

Prawn and couscous salad

This salad contains prawns, which are rich in selenium, peppers for vitamin C and seeds to give it a nice nutty flavour. Prawns are also very easy for toddlers to eat and tend to be popular.

200g couscous
25g sesame seeds
25g sunflower seeds
200g small prawns or shrimp (cooked)
½ red pepper
½ yellow pepper
½ red onion
small handful fresh parsley
small handful fresh coriander
1 lemon

Preparation time: 20 minutes.
Equipment: 1 saucepan, 1 baking tray and 1 mixing bowl.
Storage: Fridge for 24 hours.
Servings: 2 adults and 1 toddler.

- Put the couscous in a small pan, add 400ml of boiling water, then put the lid on and leave for at least 5 minutes.
- Put the seeds on a baking tray and place them under the grill for a few minutes until toasted. Stir occasionally.
- Very finely dice the peppers and onion and finely chop the herbs.
- Mix everything together in the mixing bowl. Stir in the lemon juice and zest to taste – you might not want to add it all if you have a large lemon.

Tips

- Adults may want to add some salt and black pepper.
- Instead of prawns you can use chicken or chickpeas. You can also add peas or chopped tomatoes.

Pierogi ruskie

These little Polish dumplings are filled with mashed potato and cheese, but once you've got the hang of the technique you can make pierogi with just about any filling you can think of.

For the filling:
2 baking-sized potatoes
1 onion
1 tsp olive or rapeseed oil
200g cottage cheese
30g Cheddar cheese, grated

> *(Traditionally these are made with Polish white cheese, but a mixture of cottage cheese and Cheddar is a fair substitute.)*
> *For the dough:*
> 250g plain flour
> 125–150ml warm water
> 1 tbsp oil for frying

Preparation time: 1 hour.
Equipment: 2 saucepans, 1 frying pan and 1 mixing bowl.
Storage: Fridge for 1–2 days or freeze.
Servings: 30 pierogi – toddlers might eat 2 or 3.

- Peel the potatoes, chop them into small pieces and place them in a pan with enough water to cover. Bring to the boil and simmer for 10–15 minutes until soft.
- Meanwhile, peel and dice the onion and fry it in one teaspoon of oil for about 5 minutes, until soft and slightly browned.
- To make the dough, mix the flour with the water and knead until smooth.
- Roll out the dough quite thinly (2–3mm) and cut out circles about 6cm across, using a pastry cutter or glass.
- When the potatoes are cooked, drain them and let as much water evaporate as possible.
- Mash the potatoes and add the fried onion, cottage cheese and grated Cheddar.
- To make the pierogi, take one of the circles of dough and place a teaspoonful of the potato mixture in the centre. Fold over the dough and stick the edges of the circle together with a little warm water to create a small semi-circular dumpling.
- Bring a large pan of water to the boil and add a few pierogi at a time, until they are all in. Stir to prevent them sticking together or sticking to the bottom of the pan.
- Once they have risen to the surface of the water, continue cooking for another 3 minutes, then drain.
- Heat some oil in the frying pan and fry the pierogi for a couple of minutes on each side until browned. You'll probably have to do this in two batches.

Tips

- These are usually eaten with more fried onion, sometimes with bacon too, and dipped in sour cream. You can try them this way or give them to your baby with some roasted vegetables and yogurt dip.

- In Poland, pierogi are also filled with minced beef, mushrooms and boiled or pickled cabbage, or with sweet fillings made from seasonal fruit.

Quickest ever pizza

This doesn't need to be left to rise like traditional pizza dough so you can make it in the same amount of time as it takes to get a pizza delivered. It's also a good introduction to cooking for toddlers, as it can't really go wrong.

250g self-raising flour
2 tbsp olive oil, plus extra for greasing
100ml warm water
100g passata
3 tbsp tomato purée
75g Cheddar cheese

Plus any topping you like:
spinach and ricotta (with a pinch of nutmeg)
tuna and sweetcorn
mushroom
sliced tomatoes
finely diced red or yellow peppers

Preparation time: 20 minutes plus 10–15 minutes cooking.
Equipment: 1 baking tray and 1 mixing bowl.
Storage: Best eaten straight away or fridge for 24 hours.
Servings: 2 adults and 1 toddler.

- Preheat the oven to 230°C/450°F/gas mark 8.
- Brush the baking tray with oil.
- Mix the flour, oil and water in the bowl with a spoon. Then, using your hands, knead the mixture into a ball.
- Knead the dough on a floured surface for 5 minutes, then roll it out until it is about ½cm thick and the right shape to fit your baking tray.
- Mix together the passata and tomato purée and spread it over the pizza base.
- Put on your favourite toppings, then grate the cheese over the top and put the pizza in the oven for 10–15 minutes.

Spinach and ricotta lasagne

Traditional lasagne can take an age to prepare but this version is much quicker and the all-in-one method for the sauce means you don't need to worry about lumps. It makes a perfect supper with tomato salad or cherry tomatoes cut in half.

1 tbsp butter or margarine
20g plain flour
350ml milk
1 bay leaf
175g frozen spinach (or fresh)
150g ricotta
1 tbsp parmesan or pecorino cheese, grated
¼ nutmeg, grated
150g lasagne sheets
30g cheese (mozzarella or Cheddar), grated
10g pine nuts

Preparation time: 20 minutes plus 30–40 minutes cooking.
Equipment: 1 saucepan, 1 ovenproof dish (about 2 pints/1 litre sized) and 1 hand-held blender.
Storage: Fridge for 24 hours or freeze.
Servings: 2 adults and 1 toddler.

- Preheat the oven to 190°C/375°F/gas mark 5.
- Place the butter or margarine, flour, milk and bay leaf in the pan and bring to the boil over a medium heat, stirring continuously. Then simmer for about 2 minutes on the lowest heat, still stirring.
- Put the spinach in the microwave for about 2 minutes, then, using the hand-held blender, give it a few pulses so that it is roughly chopped.
- Take the bay leaf out of the sauce and mix in the spinach, ricotta, parmesan and nutmeg.
- Put a couple of spoonfuls of the mixture in the bottom of the ovenproof dish and spread them out, then cover with a layer of lasagne. Repeat the layers of sauce and lasagne, ending with a layer of sauce.
- Sprinkle over the cheese and pine nuts and place the lasagne in the oven for 30–40 minutes.

66 *I tried the lasagne and we all loved it . . . it was easy to make and Sienna loved the pine nuts and cheese!* 99
Lauren, mum to Sienna Rose, 2 years

Vegetable and lentil bolognese

This is a very versatile dish: it can be puréed for younger babies, or the whole family can eat it with spaghetti and grated cheese. You can substitute any other vegetables you have in the fridge and it freezes very well.

1 tbsp olive oil
1 onion
½ red pepper
2 sticks celery
100g dried red lentils
1 tsp dried basil
½ tsp cinnamon
350ml water
1 × 400g tin chopped tomatoes
1 tbsp tomato purée
spaghetti or other pasta

Preparation time: 15 minutes plus 20 minutes cooking.
Equipment: 1 deep-sided frying pan with lid.
Storage: Fridge for 1–2 days or freeze.
Servings: 2 adults and 2 children.

- Cook the pasta according to instructions on the packet.
- Finely dice the onion, pepper and celery.
- Heat the oil in the frying pan and fry the vegetables for 5 minutes until softened.
- Add the lentils, basil and cinnamon and stir.
- Add the water and bring to the boil, then simmer for 15 minutes with the lid on while the lentils soften and most of the water is absorbed.
- Add the tin of tomatoes and tomato purée and stir. Turn the heat up to bring it back to the boil, then simmer for a few more minutes. Stir through the cooked pasta.

Tips

- Younger babies can have this as it is, or have the pasta whole with the sauce puréed, or both the sauce and pasta roughly mashed.

Mild chilli

This is a very mild chilli so you can introduce your toddler to the flavour without giving her something too hot and spicy.

2 tsp rapeseed oil
1 small onion
½ red pepper
200g minced lean beef or 150g soya mince or Quorn mince
½ tsp ground cumin
¼ tsp sweet paprika
pinch of mild chilli powder
½ × 400g tin kidney beans (or adzuki beans, which are similar but softer)
1 × 400g tin chopped tomatoes
1 tbsp tomato purée
½ tsp sugar

Preparation time: 40 minutes.
Equipment: 1 deep-sided frying pan with lid.
Storage: Fridge for 24 hours or freeze.
Servings: 2 adults and 1 toddler or 10 toddler portions.

- Peel and dice the onion and dice the red pepper.
- Heat the oil in the pan and sauté the onion and pepper for 5 minutes, until soft but not browned.
- Add the beef, if using, and stir with the vegetables until browned. Or add the soya or Quorn mince and just give it a stir – it doesn't need to brown but if it's frozen stir until it defrosts.
- Add the spices and cook for another minute.
- Stir in the chopped tomatoes, beans, tomato purée and sugar. Bring to the boil, then put the lid on and simmer for about 20 minutes.

Tips

- Serve with rice or wraps and maybe some lettuce or cucumber and a little grated cheese or sour cream.
- If you're using soya or Quorn mince you might like to add half a teaspoon of marmite or another yeast extract to give it more flavour.
- You can also add other vegetables such as mushrooms or courgette.

Baked fish goujons

These are great for toddlers to eat with their hands as they stay in one piece better than regular fish fingers. They're also a great substitute for older fans of fish fingers as they have more fish and less coating.

1 tsp olive or rapeseed oil
225g firm white fish (haddock, river cobbler, cod, etc.) (weight without skin)
50g plain flour
1 egg
50g polenta
1 tsp paprika

Preparation time: 15 minutes plus 10–15 minutes cooking.
Equipment: 1 baking tray and 3 bowls.
Storage: Fridge for 1–2 days or freeze before baking.
Servings: 2 adults and 1 toddler.

- Preheat the oven to 220°C/425°F/gas mark 7.
- Brush the baking tray with oil.
- Remove the skin and any bones from the fish and cut it into fish finger-sized pieces.
- Prepare three bowls: the first containing the flour, beaten egg in the second, and the polenta mixed with paprika in the third.
- Dip the pieces of fish in each one in turn and place them on the baking tray.
- Bake for 10–15 minutes, turning once halfway through.

Tips

- Serve with potato wedges or oven chips and mushy peas (see p141).
- If you would rather fry the goujons, heat a tablespoon of oil in a frying pan and cook them for about 5 minutes on each side.

Simple fried fish

This is a very easy way to cook white fish for toddlers, without any egg or milk. Grilling and baking works well for oily fish such as salmon and trout but white fish can become a little dry or too flaky for toddlers to handle. This method uses very little oil so it's still healthy.

2 tsp olive or rapeseed oil
2–3 fillets of firm white fish (haddock, river cobbler, cod, etc.)
3 tbsp plain flour
½ tsp paprika (optional)
black pepper (optional)

Preparation time: 5 minutes plus 10 minutes cooking.
Equipment: 1 large plate and 1 frying pan.
Storage: Best eaten straight away.
Servings: 2 adults and 1 toddler.

- Put the flour on the plate and mix in the paprika and black pepper, if using.
- Take a piece of fish and place it in the flour to coat, then turn over to coat the other side. Place at the side of the plate and repeat with the other fillets.
- Heat the oil in the frying pan until sizzling, then lay the fish in the pan and cook for 5 minutes on each side.
- Drain the fish on a piece of kitchen paper if it looks at all greasy.

Tips

- It's essential that the oil is sizzling before you put the fish in the pan – if not, it will be greasy rather than slightly crispy. To check that your oil is hot enough, you can drop in a small cube of bread and it should sizzle instantly.

Tuna meatballs

These are brilliant with spaghetti and can easily be eaten with hands. They're especially good for toddlers who aren't too keen on fish.

2 × 160g tins of tuna (in oil, brine or spring water)
75g wholemeal bread
1 egg
2 spring onions
1 tbsp fresh parsley
25g Cheddar cheese, grated
1 tbsp vegetable oil

Preparation time: 20 minutes.
Equipment: 1 frying pan, 1 large bowl and 1 food processor.
Storage: Fridge for 24 hours or freeze.
Servings: 12 meatballs.

- Drain the tuna and break it into flakes in the bowl with a fork.
- Turn the bread into breadcrumbs using the food processor with a chopper attachment, and add them to the tuna.
- Finely chop the spring onions and parsley and add to the mixture.
- Add the egg and grated cheese to the bowl and mix thoroughly.
- Using your hands, form the mixture into about 12 walnut-sized balls.
- Heat the oil in the frying pan until sizzling, then place the balls into the pan and cook for 5–10 minutes, turning occasionally so that they brown all over.

Tips

- Serve with spaghetti and basic tomato sauce (p38).
- To reheat the meatballs, place them on an oiled baking tray at 200°C/400°F/ gas mark 6 for 10–15 minutes.
- These can also be flattened into tuna burgers and eaten in pitta bread with some salad.

Salmon and spring onion rösti

These are super healthy, packed with long-chain omega 3s and delicious. They're also easier for babies to grasp than traditional fish cakes made with mashed potato.

2 salmon fillets (about 300g)
500g potatoes (including skins)
3 spring onions
1 egg
1–2 tbsp oil

Preparation time: 30 minutes.
Equipment: 2 frying pans or 1 frying pan and 1 baking tray (to keep the first batch warm while you cook the second), 1 mixing bowl and 1 food processor (optional).
Storage: Fridge for 24 hours or freeze. Reheated under the grill.
Servings: 12–15 rösti – enough for 2 adults and 2 children.

- Peel and grate the potatoes, either by hand or in a food processor.
- Place the grated potato on the centre of a clean tea towel. Then bring together the corners and twist tightly over the sink to remove as much water as possible.

- Remove the skin from the salmon and cut it into 1cm cubes, removing bones if you find any.
- Finely chop the spring onion.
- Mix the grated potato, salmon, spring onion and egg together in a mixing bowl.
- Heat a thin layer of oil in the frying pan over a medium heat. When it's hot, put large spoonfuls of the mixture into the pan. You should be able to make about six at a time. Squash each one down with a spatula or fish slice so that it is about 1cm thick.
- Fry the rösti gently for 5–10 minutes until nicely browned, pressing down again from time to time, then flip them over and do the same on the other side.
- Remove and drain on kitchen paper.

Tips

- Serve with salad or stir-fried vegetables.
- To make the rösti egg-free, simply leave out the egg and the recipe will still work, although they won't stay together quite so well.

> 66 *I wasn't sure what Luca would make of these as he is not keen on potatoes, but I made them quite small, they held together nicely and he enjoyed eating two with his fingers.* 99
> **Christine, mum to Luca, 3 years, and Theo, 3 months**

Paella

This is a simple version of paella, without mussels or spicy sausage, but with plenty of taste and different ingredients to keep toddlers interested.

1 tbsp olive oil
150g chicken (breast or dark meat)
1 red onion
1 garlic clove, crushed
½ yellow pepper
1 courgette
¼ tsp turmeric
1 tsp sweet paprika
150g basmati rice
1 stock cube made up with 400ml water
100g prawns
50g frozen peas
1 tbsp parsley, chopped

Preparation time: 35–40 minutes.
Equipment: 1 paella pan or 1 deep-sided frying pan with lid.
Storage: Fridge for 24 hours or freeze.
Servings: 2 adults and 1 toddler

- Chop the chicken into bite-sized pieces.
- Heat the oil in the pan and fry the chicken for 3–4 minutes until browned. Transfer to a bowl and set aside.
- Peel and dice the onion and dice the pepper and fry gently for a couple of minutes.
- Dice the courgette, add it to the pan with the garlic, and fry for 5 minutes more.
- Add the spices and stir for a minute over the heat.
- Add the rice and stir for another minute.
- Pour the stock over the rice. Bring it to the boil, then cover the pan and simmer for 10 minutes.
- Stir the chicken, prawns and peas into the rice and simmer for 5–10 minutes more, until the water is absorbed and everything is cooked through. It's fine to add the prawns and peas still frozen.
- Gently stir in the parsley and serve.

Tips

- If your baby enjoys this you could try adding other fish or seafood. You can also use different vegetables to suit your toddler's tastes or just use what you have in the fridge.

> 66 This was easy to make and a success with the whole family. It's also good with different vegetables – carrots, green beans and sweetcorn work well. 99
> **Monika, mum to Filip, 9 years, Max, 7 years, and Julian, 2 years**

One-pot chicken and couscous

This Moroccan-inspired dish is easy to make and introduces toddlers to new flavour combinations. If your baby enjoys it you can add a little more of the spices next time you cook it.

> 1 tbsp olive oil
> 200g chicken
> 1 onion
> ½ red pepper
> 2 cloves garlic, crushed
> ¼–½ tsp ground cinnamon
> ¼ tsp turmeric
> ½ tsp ground cumin
> ½ tsp ground coriander
> 1 lemon
> 1 tsp fresh ginger, grated
> 1 × 400g tin chickpeas
> 100g frozen peas
> 1 very low salt chicken or vegetable stock cube made up with 400ml
> boiling water
> 150g couscous

Preparation time: 30 minutes.
Equipment: 1 deep-sided frying pan with lid.
Storage: Fridge for 1–2 days or freeze.
Servings: 2 adults and 1 toddler or about 12 toddler portions

- Cut the chicken into cubes and leave aside.
- Peel and dice the onion and dice the pepper (or cut the pepper into thin strips for toddlers who eat with their hands).
- Heat the oil in the pan, then fry the onion, pepper and garlic for 2 minutes.
- Add the chicken and fry for 6–8 minutes, turning occasionally.
- Meanwhile, put the spices, ginger and grated lemon zest in a small bowl or cup so that they're ready and prepare the stock.
- When the chicken is cooked, add the spice mixture and fry for another minute.
- Add the peas, chickpeas, stock, lemon juice and couscous and bring to the boil.
- Put the lid on and turn off the heat. Leave for 5 minutes until the water is absorbed.

Tips

- Chicken thighs work well in this recipe – they're cheaper than chicken breast and contain up to twice as much iron.

- Traditionally, the dish would contain dried fruit such as apricots or prunes. I've left these out, as many Brits are averse to sweet–savoury combinations. However, if you're not, these can be added with the chickpeas and stock.
- Adults might want to spice up their portion with a little harissa paste.
- If you're giving this to a younger baby who hasn't had chickpeas before, you might want to squish them.
- Vegetarians can leave out the chicken and add some sweetcorn or beans instead.
- If you're unsure what lemon zest is, it's the very outside yellow part of the lemon peel. To remove it from a lemon you need a 'zester' or you can use a fine grater.

> **❝** We all enjoyed this and Ivy showed her appreciation with lots of 'mmms' and 'yumyums'. She enjoyed looking to see what different ingredients she could find on her plate. As it's quite moist it was easy for her to scoop it up with her spoon and fork. **❞**
> **Adele, mum to Ivy, 19 months**

Chicken stir-fry

This colourful stir-fry is perfect for toddlers who want to eat with their hands, but it can also be chopped up for those who prefer a spoon or fork.

1 tbsp rapeseed oil
2 chicken breasts (about 250g)
2 spring onions
½ red pepper
6 baby sweetcorn
1 carrot
100g cabbage (sweetheart or green)
1 garlic clove, crushed
2½cm fresh ginger, grated
1 tbsp rice vinegar or white wine vinegar
½ tsp ground coriander
noodles or rice

Preparation time: 30 minutes.
Equipment: 1 large frying pan or wok and 1 saucepan.
Storage: Fridge for 24 hours or freeze.
Servings: 2 adults and 1 toddler or 10–12 toddler portions.

- Cut the chicken breasts into strips.
- Heat one teaspoon of oil in the frying pan and cook the chicken for 4–5 minutes, then set aside.
- While the chicken is cooking, cut the spring onions and pepper into thin strips. Chop the baby sweetcorn in quarters lengthways. Peel the carrot and cut it into thin batons and shred the cabbage.
- Put the remaining oil in the pan with the crushed garlic, grated ginger, vinegar and coriander. Heat and stir, then add all the vegetables apart from the cabbage.
- Cook for 3–4 minutes, then add the cabbage and cook for a few minutes more.
- Put the chicken back into the pan and cook through until everything is ready. If you're having noodles, these can be added too.

Tips

- Adults might want to add soya sauce, but it is high in salt (0.6g salt per teaspoonful) so it is best not to give it to babies.
- Stir-frying is a good way of encouraging your baby to eat a wide variety of vegetables. You can try adding broccoli, mushrooms, green beans, mangetout or cauliflower.
- For a vegetarian version, leave out the chicken and cook cubes of tofu at the same time as the vegetables.

66 *This was really easy and quick, and a good way to give them lots of vegetables without them noticing. I wouldn't have thought they'd like ginger, but they didn't notice it. We all loved it and had the leftovers in wraps the next day.* 99
Tom, dad to Ellie, 5 years, and Ruthie, 3 years

Chicken and vegetable curry

This is the perfect introduction to curry as it is only mildly spicy and contains no chilli. However, it's still full of flavour so the whole family will enjoy it.

1 tbsp rapeseed oil
1 onion
2 cloves garlic, crushed
450g vegetables (e.g. carrot, aubergine, cauliflower, broccoli, squash, potato)
2 chicken breasts (about 250g)

1 tsp ground cumin
1 tsp ground coriander
1 tsp turmeric
1 × 400g tin chopped tomatoes
1 very low salt stock cube made up with 300ml water
1 tbsp tomato purée
40g creamed coconut block

Preparation time: 30 minutes plus 30 minutes cooking.
Equipment: 1 large saucepan with lid.
Storage: Fridge for 24 hours or freeze.
Servings: 2 adults and 2 toddlers

- Peel and dice the onion and other vegetables.
- Heat the oil in the pan and sauté the onion for 3–4 minutes until softened. Add the vegetables and garlic and cook with the lid on for about 10 minutes, until the vegetables are starting to become tender but aren't browned.
- Cut the chicken into bite-sized pieces.
- Turn the heat up and add the chicken. Cook, stirring for 2–3 minutes, until starting to brown.
- Add the spices and stir for a minute.
- Add the tin of tomatoes and the stock. Stir and bring to the boil, then simmer with the lid on for 20–30 minutes, until the vegetables are tender.
- Add the tomato purée and creamed coconut and continue cooking for 5 minutes, stirring occasionally.

Tips

- Serve with steamed or boiled rice, chopped fresh coriander and natural yogurt.
- If your toddler is happy with spicy food, you can use up to twice the amount of spices and even try a little chilli too.
- For a vegetarian version, leave out the chicken and add a tin of chickpeas at the same time as the tin of tomatoes.

Turkey and apple burgers

These are a great alternative to beef burgers as they contain much less saturated fat. Adding fruit to the turkey also appeals to some babies who aren't so fond of meat.

> 250g lean turkey, minced
> 1 garlic clove, crushed
> ½ small onion
> 1 eating apple
> ½ tsp dried parsley (or 1 tbsp chopped fresh parsley)
> large pinch cinnamon
> 1 tbsp rapeseed oil

Preparation time: 30 minutes.
Equipment: 1 frying pan and 1 mixing bowl.
Storage: Fridge for 24 hours or freeze raw burgers.
Servings: 2 adults and 1 toddler.

- Peel, core and coarsely grate the apple into the mixing bowl.
- Peel the onion and dice as finely as possible, then add the onion, crushed garlic, parsley, cinnamon and turkey to the bowl.
- Mix everything together with a spoon or your hands, then, using your hands, form the mixture into one large patty at the bottom of the bowl. Divide this into six to eight pieces and shape them into burgers. Smaller, flatter burgers tend to work better than thicker ones.
- Heat the oil in the frying pan over a high heat and sear the burgers for 1–2 minutes on each side to brown them. Then turn the heat down low and cook for about 5 minutes more on each side so that the turkey cooks through without burning.

Tips

- Serve in granary rolls with salad and mayonnaise or ketchup. Or have with pasta and a tomato-based sauce.

> 66 *These were a success. My daughter won't usually touch meat so it was great!* 99
> **Lauren, mum to Sienna Rose, 2 years**

Beef and bean burgers

This recipe combines two iron-rich foods: beef and kidney beans. By including the meat, iron absorption from the beans is increased. The combination also means the burgers have less saturated fat and more fibre – making them more nutritionally rounded.

½ small onion
a few fresh basil leaves (or pinch dried basil)
½ tin kidney beans (about 120g)
200g extra lean minced beef
20g oats
1 egg
1 tbsp olive oil

Preparation time: 15 minutes plus 10–15 minutes cooking.
Equipment: 1 frying pan, 1 mixing bowl and 1 hand-held blender.
Storage: Fridge for 1–2 days or freeze before cooking.
Servings: 2 adults and 1–2 toddlers.

- Peel and dice the onion and chop the basil.
- Put the onion, basil and beans in the bowl and purée slightly by giving the mixture a few quick pulses with the blender.
- Add the mince, oats and egg and give everything a good stir.
- Divide the mixture into five pieces, then shape them into burgers that are about 1cm thick and 8cm in diameter. You can put them in the fridge or freezer at this point if you want to.
- Heat the oil in a frying pan and cook the burgers over a medium heat for 5–7 minutes on each side.

Tips

- Serve with mashed sweet potato and green beans or in a wrap spread with mashed avocado along with some tomato and cucumber.
- These can be made into sausage shapes if your baby finds them easier to eat this way.

> 66 *These went down a treat. Luca is a bit fussy with meat and he doesn't normally like minced meat but with this recipe he asked for a second helping! My husband and I really enjoyed the burgers as well and we'll definitely be making them again.* 99
> **Christine, mum to Luca, 3 years, and Theo, 3 months**

Homemade ketchup

A dollop of ketchup is great with chips and can also help reluctant broccoli and cabbage eaters with their greens. Shop-bought versions are generally high in salt, and even some reduced-salt varieties contain almost a third of a baby's salt limit in just one tablespoonful. This homemade ketchup has no added salt, is easy to make and can be kept in the freezer for when it's needed.

1 tbsp olive oil
½ red onion
½ red pepper
1 × 400g tin chopped tomatoes
100g tomato purée
1 tbsp balsamic vinegar (or cider vinegar or white wine vinegar)
25g treacle
1 tbsp soft brown sugar

Preparation time: 20 minutes plus 10–15 minutes cooking.
Equipment: 1 saucepan and 1 hand-held blender.
Storage: Fridge for 3–4 days or freeze.
Servings: 20–25 portions.

- Peel and dice the onion and dice the pepper.
- Heat the oil in the saucepan and cook the onion and pepper for 5 minutes with the lid on, until softened but not browned.
- Add the rest of the ingredients, bring to the boil, then simmer for 10 minutes without a lid.
- Take the pan off the heat and purée the mixture.
- Return the mixture to the heat and cook for 5 minutes, or longer if you prefer, while the sauce thickens to a suitable consistency.
- Transfer to an ice-cube tray to cool and freeze.

Tips

- Make sure your tomato purée doesn't have any added salt, as some do.
- You can leave the sugar out, but it can mean the sauce is rather acidic. By using a heaped tablespoon of treacle you're adding sugar but also iron, so it's not all bad.
- Mix one teaspoon of ketchup with a tablespoon of yogurt to make a nice tomatoey dip for pitta bread fingers or vegetable patties.

Puddings and snacks

Toddlers sometimes yearn for more exciting puddings than fruit and yogurt, especially if they see other children tucking into a chocolate muffin or ice cream with sprinkles. Treats like this are fine occasionally, but if fruit is presented in an interesting way, for example layered with yogurt or on a skewer, it often goes down just as well. Warm puddings including rice pudding (p98) and crumble (p95) are also popular and good for everyone in the family to enjoy together.

Snacks such as those on page 150 are all good for toddlers, or if you find your child isn't eating certain foods at mealtimes, you can always serve these at snack time – for example, houmous and vegetable sticks or mini tuna sandwiches. Try to resist the lure of commercial snacks. These tend to be cheap and high in sugar and salt, or more expensive but still with added sugar, even if it's in the form of concentrated juice, honey or syrup. Shop-bought products usually taste different to homemade recipes or foods in their natural state, and they can make natural foods taste bland in comparison. Of course, there's nothing wrong with having cake sometimes, but the recipes included here are all healthier than standard ones. They also include fruit or both fruit and nuts, so they provide extra micronutrients as well as being sweet and tasty.

Fruit and chocolate fondue

The avocado in this dip can't be detected but gives it a deliciously creamy texture. It also makes it super healthy – compared with melted chocolate, this contains 80% less sugar and saturated fat and four times as much vitamin E.

1 small avocado
1½ tsp cocoa powder
2 tsp honey (or caster sugar for under-12-month-olds)
¼ tsp vanilla essence
2 tbsp milk or soya milk

Any fruit, such as:
strawberries
pineapple cubes
thick slices of banana

wedges of apple or pear
segments of satsuma

Preparation time: 5 minutes.
Equipment: 1 bowl and 1 food processor or hand-held blender.
Storage: Fridge for 24 hours or freeze for up to 2 weeks (freezing for longer may affect the colour and texture of the avocado). Defrost in the fridge.
Servings: 3–4 portions.

- Cut the avocado in half, remove the stone and scoop the flesh into the bowl.
- Add the cocoa powder, honey, vanilla essence and milk.
- Blend until smooth.

Tips

- To make a runnier dip, simply add more milk.
- Your toddler can either use her hands to dip in pieces of fruit or use a fork. Slightly older children might enjoy using a cocktail stick.

Baked apples

This is a traditional pudding, made here with less butter and sugar, but with nuts and spices instead for extra flavour.

3 eating apples
1 heaped tbsp dried mixed fruit
2 tsp dark muscovado sugar, or other brown sugar
½ tsp mixed spice or cinnamon
2 tbsp chopped nuts (e.g. pecans, hazelnuts, walnuts) (optional)
1 tsp butter or margarine

Preparation time: 10 minutes plus 30–40 minutes cooking.
Equipment: 1 ovenproof dish and 1 bowl.
Storage: Fridge for 1–2 days.
Servings: 2 adults and 2 toddlers

- Preheat the oven to 200°C/400°F/gas mark 6.
- Put the apples on a flat surface and remove the core using a potato peeler or small knife, then place them in the dish.

- Mix the dried fruit, sugar, spices and nuts in a small bowl and spoon the mixture into the centre of the apples.
- Dot the butter or margarine on top of each apple.
- Pour boiling water into the dish to form a ½cm deep layer, then place the dish in the oven for 30–40 minutes. Baste the apples with the sugary liquid occasionally.

Tips

- Serve with custard, dairy vanilla ice cream or a spoonful of crème fraîche.

Chocolate, pear and almond pudding

This pudding has a layer of pears covered with a light chocolate and almond sponge. Perfect for Sunday lunch, it can be eaten warm with vanilla ice cream or crème fraîche, or cold with hands.

4 ripe pears or 1 × 425g tin pears
100g self-raising flour
½ tsp baking powder
75g caster sugar
2 eggs
100ml rapeseed oil
25g ground almonds
1 tsp flaked almonds

Preparation time: 15 minutes plus 15–20 minutes cooking.
Equipment: 1 flan dish or similar and 1 mixing bowl or food processor.
Storage: Fridge for 1–2 days.
Servings: 8 –10 adult and child portions.

- Preheat the oven to 200°C/400°F/gas mark 6.
- Cut the pears into quarters. Remove the peel and core and cut them into chunks. Spread the chunks over the base of the flan dish.
- Put all the remaining ingredients, apart from the almonds, in a mixing bowl or food processor and whisk to form a thick batter.
- Fold in the ground almonds and spoon the mixture over the top of the pears.
- Smooth the mixture to form a fairly even layer and sprinkle over the flaked almonds.
- Bake for 15–20 minutes.

Tips

- For a nut-free version, simply leave out the ground and flaked almonds and the recipe still works perfectly.

Ginger biscuits

These are made with wholemeal flour and treacle for extra iron.

150g wholemeal flour
50g plain flour (plus extra for dusting)
2 tsp baking powder
1½ tsp ground ginger
½ tsp ground cinnamon
25g soft brown sugar
100ml rapeseed oil plus extra for greasing
1 heaped tbsp treacle
2 tbsp apple juice

Preparation time: 20 minutes plus 10 minutes cooking.
Equipment: 2 baking trays and 1 mixing bowl.
Storage: Airtight container for 2–3 days or freeze.
Servings: 24 biscuits.

- Preheat the oven to 190°C/375°F/gas mark 5.
- Grease the baking trays.
- Mix the flour, baking powder, sugar and spices together in the mixing bowl.
- Make a well in the centre of the mixture and add the oil, treacle and apple juice.
- Stir the mixture well to combine all the ingredients and form a dough.
- On a floured work surface, roll the dough to a 3–4mm thickness. Make 24 biscuits using a biscuit cutter 5½cm in diameter, re-rolling any off-cuts to use up all the dough.
- Place the biscuits on the baking trays and bake for 10 minutes.

Tips

- Treacle isn't easy to handle but the easiest way to weigh it is using electronic scales with a re-zero function. Put the tin of treacle on the scales without the lid, zero the reading, then take out the amount you need and use the same spoon for stirring the biscuit mixture.

Fruit and nut cereal bars

This is easier to make than most other cereal bar and flapjack recipes. It doesn't contain lots of butter and syrup, so it's much healthier too.

200g porridge oats
6 dried apricots
25g pumpkin seeds
25g sesame seeds
25g ground almonds
100g rapeseed oil
3 tbsp honey
2 ripe bananas

Preparation time: 15 minutes plus 20–25 minutes cooking.
Equipment: 1 baking tray (Swiss roll type, about 20cm × 30cm) and 1 mixing bowl.
Storage: Airtight container for 3–4 days or freeze.
Servings: 24 cereal bars.

- Preheat the oven to 180°C/350°F/gas mark 4.
- Cover the baking tray with a piece of greaseproof paper. This needn't be cut to size – it can stick up at the edges.
- Chop the pumpkin seeds and apricots.
- Place the oats, pumpkin seeds, apricots, sesame seeds, ground almonds, honey and oil in the mixing bowl.
- Mash the bananas and mix them with the other ingredients.
- Spoon the mixture into the prepared tin and press it down well with the back of the spoon to make an even layer.
- Bake for 20–25 minutes until golden brown.
- Take it out of the oven and mark into 24 bars.
- Leave the tray until completely cooled, then slice through and put the bars into an airtight container.

Tips

- To make these nut-free, simply leave out the almonds and the recipe will still be delicious.
- For babies under a year old, replace the honey with golden syrup.

> ❝ These have been a huge success and I'll definitely keep making them. My daughter loves them, and this is interesting as any other kind of flapjack I've tried to make for her she hasn't liked. ❞
> **Jessica, mum to Freya, 2 years**

Rock cakes

There are lots of variations on this recipe – some contain no sugar and only wholemeal flour and taste a bit 'worthy'. This version has less sugar and butter than many others, and more fruit, but still feels like a sweet treat.

225g flour (half plain and half wholemeal, or according to taste)
2 tsp baking powder
75g butter or margarine plus extra for greasing
75g demerara sugar
125g mixed dried fruit
zest of one lemon
1 egg
4–6 tbsp milk

Preparation time: 15 minutes plus 15–20 minutes cooking.
Equipment: 1 baking tray and 1 mixing bowl.
Storage: Airtight container for 1–2 days or freeze.
Servings: 12–16 cakes

- Preheat the oven to 200°C/400°F/gas mark 6.
- Grease the baking tray.
- Place the flour and baking powder in the bowl and rub in the butter or margarine until the mixture resembles fine breadcrumbs.
- Stir in the sugar, dried fruit and lemon zest.
- Make a well in the centre of the dry ingredients and add the egg and milk. Stir well.
- Using two spoons, scoop egg-sized dollops onto the tray a few centimetres apart.
- Bake for 15–20 minutes until golden brown.

Tips

- Fans of Kipper the Dog might like to add a few chopped glacé cherries to make 'Kipper cakes'.

Apple and prune drop cakes

These cakes are egg-free and sweetened with treacle instead of sugar for extra iron.

100g wholemeal flour
125g plain flour
3tsp baking powder
½ tsp mixed spice
50ml rapeseed oil plus extra for greasing
50ml milk
2 tbsp treacle
1 tbsp soft brown sugar
1 apple
75g prunes (dried, ready to eat)

Preparation time: 20 minutes plus 10–15 minutes cooking.
Equipment: 1 baking tray and 1 mixing bowl.
Storage: Airtight container for 2–3 days or freeze.
Servings: 16 cakes.

- Preheat the oven to 200°C/400°F/gas mark 6.
- Brush your baking tray with oil.
- Mix the flours, baking powder, mixed spice, sugar, oil, milk and treacle in the mixing bowl.
- Peel, core and grate the apple and chop the prunes, then mix them thoroughly with the other ingredients.
- Place spoonfuls of the mixture on the baking tray and bake for 10–15 minutes.

Date and walnut loaf

This is a rich, moist cake that is sweetened with a banana instead of sugar. The walnuts provide magnesium, which is an essential mineral for bone growth.

150g dried dates
200ml water
1 tsp bicarbonate of soda
150g plain flour
50g wholemeal flour

75ml rapeseed oil plus extra for greasing
2 eggs
1 banana
1 tsp vanilla essence
100g walnuts

Preparation time: 25 minutes plus 50 minutes–1 hour baking.
Equipment: 1 saucepan, 1 900g loaf tin and 1 mixing bowl.
Storage: Airtight container for 1–2 days or freeze.
Servings: 14–18 slices of cake.

- Preheat the oven to 180°C/350°F/gas mark 4.
- Grease the loaf tin and sprinkle with flour.
- Put the dates, water and bicarbonate of soda in a pan. Bring to the boil, then turn off the heat and leave to soak.
- Chop the walnuts.
- Mash the banana in the mixing bowl, then stir in the oil, vanilla essence and eggs, followed by the two flours.
- Mash the dates in the pan with a fork to break them up.
- Fold the date mixture and the walnuts into the other ingredients and pour the complete mixture into the loaf tin.
- Bake for 50 minutes to 1 hour, until a skewer inserted into the centre of the loaf comes out clean. If the cake starts to brown too soon, cover it loosely with foil.

Tips

- If you find the cake isn't sweet enough, add 50g of caster sugar along with the flour.

Pineapple and coconut cake

A light, moist cake that introduces your toddler to new flavours.

400g self-raising flour
2 tsp baking powder
100g soft brown sugar
100g desiccated coconut
100g raisins
250g carrot (peeled weight)

1 × 430g tin crushed pineapple in fruit juice (280g drained)
100ml rapeseed oil
2 eggs
oil for greasing

Preparation time: 30 minutes plus 40–45 minutes cooking.
Equipment: 20cm × 30cm cake tin and 1 mixing bowl.
Storage: Airtight container for 2–3 days or freeze.
Servings: A large cake, good for a family gathering or for cutting into quarters and freezing.

- Preheat the oven to 180°C/350°F/gas mark 4.
- Grease the cake tin and line the bottom with greaseproof paper.
- In a bowl, mix the flour, baking powder, sugar, coconut and raisins.
- Peel and grate the carrots into the bowl and mix.
- Drain the pineapple and set the juice aside as this is not needed.
- In a small bowl or measuring jug, beat the eggs into the oil.
- Make a well in the centre of the flour mixture and add the crushed pineapple and the eggs mixture.
- Combine all the ingredients well and transfer to the prepared cake tin.
- Bake for 40–45 minutes, until a skewer inserted in the centre of the cake comes out dry.

Tips

- Instead of making a large cake, you can make two smaller ones or use paper cases and make muffins.
- The advantage of a large cake over individual ones is that smaller slices can be cut for smaller members of the family. They may be reluctant to accept half a muffin when other people are having a whole one, but are less likely to notice different-sized slices, at least for a couple of years.

Fruit smoothies, shakes and lassis

There are endless possibilities when it comes to smoothies, shakes and lassis, so as well as trying these recipes, experiment with creating your own with whatever you have in the fruit bowl. They are great for a weekend breakfast or you can pour them into ice-lolly moulds and make fruity lollies. Toddlers can also get involved with putting the fruit into the blender or smoothie maker, carefully supervised of course.

Fruit in a form that you can drink is ideal for toddlers who refuse to eat it in its natural state, or as a breakfast for those who've decided they'd rather not eat in the morning.

Banana lassi

1 banana (or try strawberries or mango)
3 tbsp natural yogurt
100ml milk
pinch of cinnamon

Preparation time: 5 minutes.
Equipment: 1 blender jug or hand-held blender with beaker.
Storage: Best drunk fresh.
Servings: 2 toddler portions.

- Peel and slice the banana into the jug or beaker.
- Add the yogurt and milk and blend until smooth.
- Pour into cups and sprinkle with cinnamon.

> 66 *My daughter loves fruit but isn't keen on yogurt or cheese, so I think these were a good way for her to have some calcium. As she loves ice cubes, I froze the smoothie and chopped it up and this really appealed to her.* 99
> **Sarah, mum to Lara, 16 months**

These alternatives can all be made in the same way.

Peanut butter and banana milkshake

1 banana
1 tbsp peanut butter (smooth or crunchy is fine)
100ml milk

Strawberry smoothie

6 strawberries
½ banana
100ml pressed apple juice

Melon and kiwi smoothie

100g honeydew melon
2 kiwi fruit
75ml apple juice

This one is best made in a food processor or smoothie maker, as a hand-held blender may not break up the seeds of the kiwi fruit. Some toddlers don't mind the tiny seeds but they can put others off.

Homemade ice lollies

For a delicious summer treat, use any of the above smoothie recipes and turn them into ice lollies by pouring the mixture into ice-lolly moulds and freezing for about 24 hours. To get the lollies out, run the bottom of the tray under warm water.

Meal plan for a toddler

The five-day meal plan below shows how a 1-year-old can meet all her nutrient requirements. In addition to the food, toddlers should have 300–350ml whole cows' milk (or be breastfed). They should also have vitamin drops to ensure they get enough vitamin D (p12), as cows' milk does not have added vitamin D, unlike formula. Meals and snacks now look more like those an adult would eat and each one should be given with a cup of water.

Just like the previous meal plans, this one is simply to show what a healthy diet could look like. You don't need to follow it exactly. It doesn't contain any purées or mashed meals (apart from fruit purée in yogurt as an alternative to flavoured yogurt). It also includes more bread, which should usually be granary or wholemeal. In addition, snacks are slightly more substantial to help fuel toddler activity between meals. The plan includes recipes from previous sections as well as new ones from this chapter.

Weaning Made Easy Recipes

Day	Breakfast	Snack	Lunch	Snack	Dinner
1	Blueberry breakfast cake (p159)	Banana	Granary toast with sardine pâté (p161) and sliced tomato	Ginger biscuit (p188)	One-pot chicken and couscous (p177) Chocolate fondue (p185) with peach
2	Shreddies and a banana	Blueberry breakfast cake (p159)	Cold leftover one-pot chicken and couscous (p177) with cucumber wedges Plum	Rice cakes with peanut butter	Spaghetti with vegetable and lentil bolognese (p171) and grated Cheddar Chocolate fondue (p185) with kiwi and apple
3	Scrambled eggs (p45) on toast Satsuma	Oatcake with cream cheese	Houmous and grated carrot sandwich Grapes (halved)	Ginger biscuit (p188)	Quorn mild chilli (p172) with rice and grated cheese Apple and mango purée (p51) with natural yogurt
4	Homemade muesli (p158)	Pear	Leek and pea patties (p116) and roast cauliflower (p37) with houmous	½ a cream cheese and avocado sandwich	Fish and tomato pie (p84) with broccoli Apricot rice pudding (p98)

5	Homemade muesli (p158) with strawberries	Fruit and nut cereal bar (p189)	Grated cheese and apple on toast Satsuma	Breadsticks and raisins	Beef and bean burgers (p182) with sweet potato wedges and green beans Chocolate, pear and almond pudding (p187)

This meal plan meets the requirements for energy, protein, potassium, calcium, magnesium, phosphorus, iron, copper, zinc, chloride, selenium, iodine, thiamin, riboflavin, niacin, folic acid and vitamins A, B6, B12, C and E. It also contains less than 2g of salt per day, which is the maximum toddlers should have.

Dos, don'ts and FAQs for your toddler

Do

- Eat the same food as your toddler at the same time. You're the biggest role model she has.
- Encourage your toddler to feed herself.
- Keep introducing new foods and flavours for as long as possible.
- Try to offer balanced meals even if the number of foods is limited (e.g. carrots every day is better than no vegetables).
- Offer three meals a day and no more than two small healthy snacks.

Don't

- Give too many snacks between meals, even if meals aren't eaten.
- Share salty foods you're eating such as olives, bacon, smoked salmon or ready meals.
- Worry if your toddler seems to have gone off her food – just keep offering food in the same way.

- Play games or get into battles to encourage your toddler to eat up.
- Give your toddler too much milk.

FAQs

Q: Can my child have semi-skimmed milk now?

A: Between the ages of 12 and 24 months, breast milk or whole cows' milk (full-fat) is recommended. One-year-olds can have formula milk but if they are eating reasonably well this isn't necessary. They shouldn't be given semi-skimmed milk as it doesn't have enough calories or vitamins to meet the needs of children this age. Between the ages of 2 and 5 years they can switch to semi-skimmed milk, but they shouldn't have skimmed or 1% milk as these don't provide the calories and vitamins that pre-school children need.

Q: When my daughter was younger she ate so well but now she's really fussy. Why?

A: Becoming more choosy about food is part of a toddler's way of asserting her independence. If she refuses to eat something and you try to cajole her, it can end up as a battle and make her even more determined to resist. The best thing to do is try to ignore it. This can be very difficult if she's always loved fish pie, broccoli or whatever it is you've cooked, and then she refuses to even try it. However, maybe she's just feeling under the weather or doesn't fancy it today. If you make an issue of it, then she's less likely to eat it next time, even if she's feeling well and might otherwise have enjoyed it.

It may also be that she doesn't need as much food as you think – toddlers don't grow as quickly as babies so their appetites don't keep increasing at the same rate. It is also possible that she is finding it quite fun not to eat something, because she gets lots of attention and you put on a little performance to jolly her along. The best thing to do to increase the chances of her eating a proper meal is to keep giving her a variety of healthy foods in a neutral manner and make sure she's not too full of milk, juice or snacks.

Q: If my child doesn't eat, should I give her some milk to make up for it?

A: We have an image of milk as the perfect food for little ones, and many parents feel that there's no such thing as too much. But there is. If your toddler doesn't eat a meal, then it's not a good idea to give her milk instead. She needs just over half a pint (300–350ml) a day, and any more will dull her appetite and mean she's less hungry for the next meal. It's very easy to fall into this pattern and it can make for an easy life, but it's not a good idea. Having a high milk intake has been found to increase the risk of anaemia at this age, as it means children miss out on iron-rich foods they should be having.

Q: My daughter has diarrhoea all the time. What can I do?

A: This could be 'toddler diarrhoea', but if she has other symptoms too or you suspect an allergy, then it's important to see your doctor. Children with toddler diarrhoea usually poo at least three times a day, and it is typically pale and contains bits of undigested food, particularly vegetables. It doesn't usually cause a lot of stress apart from a sore bottom. It is thought to be caused by an imbalance in the amounts of fluid, fibre and undigested food and sugar in the large bowel. It usually corrects itself by school, but dietary changes often solve the problem completely or improve it considerably.

Firstly, cut out all fruit juice and squash, or reduce it as much as possible, as the sugars in juice can contribute to the problem. Avoid clear apple juice in particular and switch to pressed cloudy apple juice if necessary. Next, make sure she's having some fibre but not too much, as both extremes can cause problems. For example, give fruit, vegetables and brown bread but not bran flakes or brown rice or wholewheat pasta. It's also important to make sure her diet isn't too low in fat. She should have full-fat milk and dairy foods. Finally, giving a probiotic may help, for example a yogurt, yogurt drink or suitable supplement.

List of recipes with dietary restrictions

Y – Yes, it's suitable for this kind of diet.
N – It's not suitable for this kind of diet. However, it may be easy to adapt, for example by using gluten-free pasta or lactose-free formula. Recipes marked with an asterisk (*) give instructions on how to adapt.

Note: Wheat-free recipes may still contain gluten, for example from oats. If you are following a wheat-free or gluten-free diet, make sure you choose suitable stock cubes and baking powder. For dairy-free versions, make sure you buy dairy-free margarine.

Chapter 2: Feeding your 4- to 6-month-old

Recipe	Dairy-free	Egg-free	Wheat-free	Nut-free	Vegetarian
Porridge fingers	N	Y	Y	Y	Y
Polenta pancakes	N	N	Y	Y	Y
Egg-free banana pancakes	N	Y	N	Y	Y
Simple vegetable or fruit purée	Y	Y	Y	Y	Y
Roasted butternut squash and red pepper purée	Y	Y	Y	Y	Y
Sweet potato and avocado	Y	Y	Y	Y	Y

Recipe	Dairy-free	Egg-free	Wheat-free	Nut-free	Vegetarian
Cauliflower, potato and chive mash	Y	Y	Y	Y	Y
Courgette, parsnip and pea purée	Y	Y	Y	Y	Y
Spinach, pea and potato purée	N	Y	Y	Y	Y
Steamed or boiled vegetable sticks	Y	Y	Y	Y	Y
Roast carrot and parsnip fingers	Y	Y	Y	Y	Y
Roasted butternut squash with ginger	Y	Y	Y	Y	Y
Baked asparagus	Y	Y	Y	Y	Y
Roast cauliflower	Y	Y	Y	Y	Y
Basic tomato sauce	Y	Y	Y	Y	Y
Tagliatelle with green sauce	N	N	N	Y	Y
Red pepper and polenta soldiers	N	Y	Y	Y	Y
Couscous patties	N	N	N	Y	Y
Avocado and yogurt dip	N	Y	Y	Y	Y
Bean purée	Y	Y	Y	Y	Y
Yellow split pea dhal	Y	Y	Y	Coconut	Y
Scrambled eggs	N	N	Y	Y	Y
Haddock and sweet potato	Y	Y	Y	Y	N
Chicken and vegetable purée	Y	Y	Y	Y	N
Chicken and vegetable fingers	Y	Y	Y	Y	N
Baby beef stew	Y	Y	Y	Y	N
Pork and apple with rice	Y	Y	Y	Y	N

Continued over page

Continued from overleaf

Recipe	Dairy-free	Egg-free	Wheat-free	Nut-free	Vegetarian
Apple and mango purée	Y	Y	Y	Y	Y
Banana and blueberry purée	Y	Y	Y	Y	Y
Pear and sultana purée	Y	Y	Y	Y	Y
Apple, apricot and banana	Y	Y	Y	Y	Y
Apple and squash dessert	N	Y	Y	Y	Y
Blueberry delight	N	Y	Y	Y	Y
Peachy pudding	N	Y	Y	Y	Y

Chapter 3: Feeding your 7- to 9-month-old

Recipe	Dairy-free	Egg-free	Wheat-free	Nut-free	Vegetarian
Fruit and nut porridge	N	Y	Y	N*	Y
Eggy bread soldiers	N	N	N	Y	Y
Salmon pâté	N	Y	Y	Y	N
Butter bean and parsley pâté	N*	Y	Y	Y	Y
Butternut squash and sage dip	N	Y	Y	Y	Y
Soya bean and pea houmous	N*	Y	Y	Y	Y
Wraps	Y	Y	N	Y	Y
Corn flatbreads	Y	Y	Y	Y	Y
Cream of vegetable soup	N	Y	N	Y	Y
Baked courgette fingers	N	N	Y	Y	Y
Parsnip fritters	N	N	N	Y	Y
Falafel	Y	Y	N	Y	Y
Yogurt dressing	N	Y	Y	Y	Y

Recipe	Dairy-free	Egg-free	Wheat-free	Nut-free	Vegetarian
Baked aubergine and lentils	Y	Y	Y	Y	Y
Vegetarian cottage pie with sweet potato mash	N*	Y	Y	Y	Y
Lentil and vegetable cobbler	N	N*	N	Y	Y
Macaroni cheese	N	Y	N	Y	Y
Cheese and chive oven omelette	N	N	Y	Y	Y
Tomato and mushroom tortilla	Y	N	Y	Y	Y
Cod with sweet peppers	Y	Y	Y	Y	N
Grilled fish with watercress sauce	N	Y	Y	Y	N
Fish and tomato pie	N	Y	Y	Y	N
Mackerel and tomato pasta sauce	Y	Y	N	Y	N
Pasta with chicken and broccoli	N	Y	N	N	N
Mini pork and apple patties	N	Y	N	Y	N
Chicken and spring vegetable one-pot	N	Y	N	Y	N
Lamb shank with tomato and rosemary	Y	Y	N	Y	N
Baked Roman gnocchi	N	N	N	Y	Y
Bubble and squeak cakes	Y	Y	N	Y	Y
Celeriac champ	N	Y	Y	Y	Y
Yorkshire pudding	N	N	N	Y	Y
Nutty apple crumble	Y	Y	N	N	Y

Continued over page

Weaning Made Easy Recipes

Continued from overleaf

Recipe	Dairy-free	Egg-free	Wheat-free	Nut-free	Vegetarian
Mango and coconut rice	Y	Y	Y	Coconut	Y
Chocolate rice pudding	N	Y	Y	Y	Y
Apricot rice pudding	N	Y	Y	Y	Y
Tropical fruit salad	Y	Y	N	Y	Y
Cheese and tomato scone biscuits	N	N*	N	Y	Y
Chocolate and Brazil nut scone biscuits	N	N*	N	N*	Y
Cheesy corn muffins	N	N	N	Y	Y
Choconana buns	Y	N	N	Y	Y

Chapter 4: Feeding your 10- to 12-month-old

Recipe	Dairy-free	Egg-free	Wheat-free	Nut-free	Vegetarian
Scotch pancakes	N	N	N*	Y	Y
Apple and sultana overnight muesli	N	Y	Y	Y	Y
Breakfast couscous	N	Y	N	Y	Y
Chickpea and rice batons	Y	N	Y	Y	Y
Leek and pea patties	Y	N	N	Y	Y
Cauliflower pizza bites	N	N	Y	Y	Y
Peanut butter burger	N	Y	N	N	Y
Beetroot dip	N*	Y	Y	Y	Y
Beany dip	N	Y	Y	N	Y
Aubergine dip	N	Y	Y	Y	Y
Red lentil soup	Y	Y	Y	Y	Y
Thick leek and potato soup	N	Y	Y	Y	Y
Easy pasta and adzuki bean salad	N	Y	N	Y	Y

List of recipes with dietary restrictions

Recipe	Dairy-free	Egg-free	Wheat-free	Nut-free	Vegetarian
Bean sausages	Y	N	N	N	Y
Mushroom loaf	N	Y	N	Y	Y
Japanese tofu patties	Y	N	Y	Y	Y
Rice with butternut squash and chickpeas	Y	Y	Y	Y	Y
Broccoli pesto	N	Y	N	Pine nuts	Y
Pasta with creamy tomato and butter bean sauce	N*	Y	N	Y	Y
Tuna carbonara	N	Y	N	Y	N
Salmon and oat patties	Y	N	Y	Y	N
Moroccan sardine balls in tomato sauce	Y	Y	Y	Y	N
Egg fried rice	Y	N	Y	Y	N*
Sage and onion sausages	Y	Y	N	Y	N
Meatballs	Y	N	Y	Y	N
Minced lamb hotpot	Y	Y	Y	Y	N
Sweet potato gnocchi	Y	N	N	Y	Y
Potato farls	N*	Y	N	Y	Y
Soft polenta	N	Y	Y	Y	Y
Mushy peas	N	Y	Y	Y	Y
Raspberry clafoutis	N	N	N	Y	Y
Cheats' cheesecake	N	Y	N	Y	Y
Fruity oat cookies	N	N	N	Y	Y
Butternut squash and ginger cake	N*	N	N	N	Y
Hot milk buns	N	Y	N	Y	Y

Continued over page

Continued from overleaf

Recipe	Dairy-free	Egg-free	Wheat-free	Nut-free	Vegetarian
Sweet potato and raisin muffins	N	N	N	Y	Y
First birthday carrot cake	N	N	N*	Y	Y

Chapter 5: Feeding your toddler and beyond

Recipe	Dairy-free	Egg-free	Wheat-free	Nut-free	Vegetarian
Homemade muesli	Y	Y	N*	N*	Y
Blueberry breakfast cake	N	N	N*	Y	Y
Sardine pâté	N	Y	Y	Y	N
Mushroom and watercress pâté	N	Y	Y	Y	Y
Tuna melt wraps	N	Y	N	Y	N
Mushroom melt	N	Y	N	Y	Y
Salmon and apple toast topper	N	Y	N	Y	N
Trout pasta salad	N*	Y	N	Y	N
Prawn couscous salad	Y	Y	N	Y	N
Pierogi ruskie	N	Y	N	Y	Y
Quickest ever pizza	N	Y	N	Y	Y
Spinach and ricotta lasagne	N	N	N	Pine nuts	Y
Vegetable and lentil bolognese	Y	Y	N	Y	Y
Mild chilli	Y	Y	Y	Y	N*
Baked fish goujons	Y	N	N	Y	N
Simple fried fish	Y	Y	N	Y	N
Tuna meatballs	N	N	N	Y	N
Salmon and spring onion rösti	Y	N	Y	Y	N

Recipe	Dairy-free	Egg-free	Wheat-free	Nut-free	Vegetarian
Paella	Y	Y	Y	Y	N
One-pot chicken and couscous	Y	Y	N	Y	N
Chicken stir-fry	Y	Y	Y	Y	N
Chicken and vegetable curry	Y	Y	Y	Coconut	N*
Turkey and apple burgers	Y	Y	Y	Y	N
Beef and bean burgers	Y	N	Y	Y	N
Homemade ketchup	Y	Y	Y	Y	Y
Fruit and chocolate fondue	N*	Y	Y	Y	Y
Baked apples	N*	Y	Y	N	Y
Chocolate, pear and almond pudding	Y	N	N	N*	Y
Ginger biscuits	Y	Y	N	Y	Y
Fruit and nut cereal bars	Y	Y	Y	N	Y
Rock cakes	N	N	N	Y	Y
Apple and prune drop cakes	N	Y	N	Y	Y
Date and walnut loaf	Y	N	N	N	Y
Pineapple and coconut cake	Y	N	N	Coconut	Y
Banana lassi	N	Y	Y	Y	Y
Peanut butter and banana milkshake	N	Y	Y	N	Y
Strawberry smoothie	Y	Y	Y	Y	Y
Melon and kiwi smoothie	Y	Y	Y	Y	Y
Homemade ice lollies	Y	Y	Y	Y	Y

Index

adzuki beans

    Easy pasta and adzuki bean salad 124

    Mild chilli 172

allergies 13, 17–18, 22, 60, 200–7

almonds

    Chocolate, pear and almond pudding
        187–8

apples

    Apple and mango purée 51

    Apple and prune drop cakes 191

    Apple and squash dessert 54

    Apple and sultana overnight muesli
        112–13

    Apple, apricot and banana 53

    Baked apples 186–7

    Mini pork and apple patties
        88–9

    Nutty apple crumble 95–6

    Pork and apple with rice 50

    Salmon and apple toast topper 164–5

    Turkey and apple burgers 181–2

apricots, dried

    Apple, apricot and banana purée 53

    Apricot rice pudding 98–9

asparagus

    Baked asparagus 37

aubergines

    Aubergine dip 121–2

    Baked aubergine and lentils 76–7

avocado

    Avocado and yogurt dip 43

    Fruit and chocolate fondue 185–6

    Salmon pâté 67–8

    Sweet potato and avocado 31–2

Baby beef stew 49

baby-led weaning (BLW) 3–5, 25–6

Baked apples 186–7

Baked asparagus 37

Baked aubergine and lentils 76–7

Baked courgette fingers 73–4

Baked fish goujons 173

Baked Roman gnocchi 91–2

bananas

    Apple, apricot and banana 53

    Banana and blueberry purée 52

    Banana lassi 194

    Choconana buns 102–3

    Egg-free banana pancakes 28–9

    Fruit and nut cereal bars 189–90

    Peachy pudding 55–6

    Peanut butter and banana milkshake
        194

    Pear and banana purée 52–3

Basic tomato sauce 38–9

Bean purée 43–4

Bean sausages 125–6

Beany dip 120–1

beef

    Baby beef stew 49

    Beef and bean burgers 182–3

    Meatballs 137

    Mild chilli 172

Beetroot dip 120

blueberries

    Banana and blueberry purée 52

    Blueberry breakfast cake 159–60

    Blueberry delight 55

Cheats' cheesecake 143–4

Brazil nuts

Chocolate and Brazil nut scone biscuits
100–1

breakfasts

Blueberry breakfast cake 159–60

Breakfast couscous 113–14

recipes 26–9, 64–7, 107–8, 111–14, 157–160,

broccoli

Broccoli pesto 129–30

Pasta with chicken and broccoli 87–8

Tagliatelle with green sauce 39–40

Bubble and squeak cakes 92–3

butter beans

Butter bean and parsley pâté 68–9

Pasta with creamy tomato and butter
bean sauce 130–1

butternut squash

Apple and squash dessert 54

Butternut squash and ginger cake 145–6

Butternut squash and sage dip 69

Rice with butternut squash and
chickpeas 128–9

Roasted butternut squash and red
pepper purée 29–30

Roasted butternut squash with ginger
36–7

cakes

Apple and prune drop cakes 191

Blueberry breakfast cake 159–60

Butternut squash and ginger cake
145–6

Choconana buns 102–3

Date and walnut loaf 191–2

First birthday carrot cake 149–50

Hot milk buns 146–7

Pineapple and coconut cake 192–3

Rock cakes 190

Sweet potato and raisin muffins 147–8

carrots

First birthday carrot cake 149–50

Pineapple and coconut cake 192–3

Roast carrot and parsnip fingers 35–6

Steamed or boiled vegetable sticks 35

cauliflower

Cauliflower pizza bites 118–19

Cauliflower, potato and chive mash 32–3

Roast cauliflower 37–8

Celeriac champ 93–4

Cheats' cheesecake 143–4

cheese

Cauliflower pizza bites 118–19

Cheese and chive oven omelette 81–2

Cheese and tomato scone biscuits 100

Cheesy corn muffins 101–2

Macaroni cheese 80–1

Mushroom melt 163

Pierogi ruskie 167–9

Quickest ever pizza 169–70

Spinach and ricotta lasagne 170

Tuna melt wraps 162–3

see also cottage cheese, ricotta

chicken

Chicken and spring vegetable
one-pot 89–90

Chicken and vegetable curry 180–1

Chicken and vegetable fingers 48–9

Chicken and vegetable purée 47–8

Chicken stir-fry 179–80

Egg fried rice 134–5

One-pot chicken and couscous 177–9

Paella 176–7

Pasta with chicken and broccoli 87–8

chickpeas

Chickpea and rice batons 115–16

Falafel 75–6

One-pot chicken and couscous 177–9

Rice with butternut squash and
chickpeas 128–9

chocolate
  Chocolate and Brazil nut scone biscuits
    100–1
  Chocolate, pear and almond pudding
    187–8
  Chocolate rice pudding 97–8
  Choconana buns 102–3
  Fruit and chocolate fondue 185–6
choking 17, 57
  see also gagging
coconut
  Mango and coconut rice 96–7
  Pineapple and coconut cake 192–3
Cod with sweet peppers 83
Corn flatbreads 71–2
cottage cheese
  Pierogi ruskie 167–9
courgettes
  Baked courgette fingers 73–4
  Courgette, parsnip and pea purée 33
  Tagliatelle with green sauce 39–40
couscous
  Breakfast couscous 113–14
  Couscous patties 41–3
  One-pot chicken and couscous
    177–9
  Prawn and couscous salad 166–7
cream cheese
  Butternut squash and sage dip 69
  Cauliflower pizza bites 118–19
  Mushroom and watercress
    pâté 161–2
  Peanut butter burger 119
Cream of vegetable soup 72–3

Date and Walnut loaf 191–2
dips 115
dried fruit
  Baked apples 186–7
  Hot milk buns 146–7
  Rock cakes 190
  see also apricots, dried; raisins; sultanas

Easy pasta and adzuki bean salad 124
Egg-free banana pancakes 28–9
eggs
  Cheese and chive oven omelette 81–2
  Egg fried rice 134–5
  Eggy bread soldiers 66
  Japanese tofu patties 127–8
  Leek and pea patties 116–18
  Polenta pancakes 27–8
  Raspberry clafoutis 142–3
  Scotch pancakes 111–12
  Scrambled eggs 45–6
  Tomato and mushroom tortilla 82–3

Falafel 75–6
finger foods 25–6, 61–2, 64, 108–9
  for dipping 114–15
  for eating out 153
  meat as 89
First birthday carrot cake 149–50
fish
  Baked fish goujons 173
  Fish and tomato pie 84–6
  Simple fried fish 173–4
  see also cod; haddock; mackerel; salmon;
    sardines; trout; tuna
flageolet beans
  Bean purée 43–4
food hygiene 16
fromage frais
  Blueberry breakfast cake 159–60
  Salmon pâté 67–8
Fruit and chocolate fondue 185–6
Fruit and nut cereal bars 189–90
Fruit and nut porridge 65–6
fruit, raw 56–7
Fruity oat cookies 144–5

gagging 17, 106–7
   see also choking
ginger
   Butternut squash and ginger cake 145–6
   Ginger biscuits 188
   Roasted butternut squash with
      ginger 36–7
Grilled fish with watercress
    sauce 84

Haddock and sweet potato 46–7
Homemade ice lollies 195
Homemade ketchup 183–4
Homemade muesli 158–9
Hot milk buns 146–7
houmous
   Soya bean and pea houmous
     69–70

Japanese tofu patties 127–8

kidney beans
   Beany dip 120–1
   Beef and bean burgers 182–3
   Mild chilli 172

kiwi fruit
   Melon and kiwi smoothie 195

lamb
   Lamb shank with tomato and rosemary
     90–1
   Minced lamb hotpot 137–9
leeks
   Leek and pea patties 116–18
   Thick leek and potato soup 123–4
lentils
   Baked aubergine and lentils 76–7
   Lentil and vegetable cobbler
     78–80

Red lentil soup 122–3
Vegetable and lentil bolognese 171
Vegetarian cottage pie with sweet
   potato mash 77–8

Macaroni cheese 80–1
Mackerel and tomato pasta 86–7
mangoes
   Apple and mango purée 51
   Mango and coconut rice 96–7
   Tropical fruit salad 99
Meatballs 137
Melon and kiwi smoothie 195
Mild chilli 172
Minced lamb hotpot 137–9
Mini pork and apple patties 88–9
Moroccan sardine balls in tomato sauce
   133–4
mushrooms
   Mushroom and watercress pâté
    161–2
   Mushroom loaf 126–7
   Mushroom melt 163
   Tomato and mushroom tortilla 82–3
Mushy peas 141–2

Nutty apple crumble 95–6

oats
   Apple and sultana overnight muesli
    112–13
   Chicken and vegetable fingers 48–9
   Fruit and nut porridge 65–6
   Fruity oat cookies 144–5
   Homemade muesli 158–9
   Porridge fingers 26–7
   Salmon and oat patties 132–3
One-pot chicken and couscous 177–9

Paella 176–7

Index

pancakes
    Egg-free banana pancakes 28–9
    Polenta pancakes 27–8
    Scotch pancakes 111–12
Steamed or boiled vegetable sticks 35
parsnips
    Courgette, parsnip and pea purée 33
    Parsnip fritters 74–5
    Roast carrot and parsnip fingers 35–6
    Steamed or boiled vegetable sticks 35
pasta
    Broccoli pesto 129–30
    Easy pasta and adzuki bean salad 124
    leftover 125
    Macaroni cheese 80–1
    Mackerel and tomato pasta 86–7
    Pasta with chicken and broccoli 87–8
    Pasta with creamy tomato and butter
        bean sauce 130–1
    Spinach and ricotta lasagne 170
    Tagliatelle with green sauce 39–40
    Trout pasta salad 165–6
    Tuna carbonara 131–2
    Vegetable and lentil bolognese 171
peaches
    Peachy pudding 55–6
    Tropical fruit salad 99
peanut butter
    Peanut butter and banana milkshake
        194
    Peanut butter burger 119
pears
    Chocolate, pear and almond pudding
        187–8
    Pear and banana purée 52–3
    Pear and sultana purée 52–3
peas
    Courgette, parsnip and pea purée 33
    Leek and pea patties 116–18
    Mushy peas 141–2

Soya bean and pea houmous
    69–70
    Spinach, pea and potato purée 33–4
Pierogi ruskie 167–9
pineapple
    Pineapple and coconut cake 192–3
    Tropical fruit salad 99
polenta
    Polenta pancakes 27–8
    Red pepper and polenta soldiers 40–1
    Soft polenta 141
pork
    Mini pork and apple patties 88–9
    Pork and apple with rice 50
    Sage and onion sausages 135–6
Porridge fingers 26–7
portion sizes 18, 22, 59–60, 198
potatoes
    Bubble and squeak cakes 92–3
    Cauliflower, potato and chive
        mash 32–3
    Celeriac champ 93–4
    Fish and tomato pie 84–6
    Minced lamb hotpot 137–9
    Pierogi ruskie 167–9
    Potato farls 140
    Salmon and spring onion rösti
        175–6
    Spinach, pea and potato purée 33–4
    Thick leek and potato soup 123–4
prawns
    Egg fried rice 134–5
    Paella 176–7
    Prawn and couscous salad 166–7
prunes
    Apple and prune drop cakes 191
puddings (deserts)
    Apricot rice pudding 97–8
    Chocolate, pear and almond pudding
        187–8

Chocolate rice pudding 98–9
Peachy pudding 55–6
recipes 50–7, 95–103, 142–50, 185–93

Quickest ever pizza 169–70

raisins
Sweet potato and raisin muffins 147–8
raspberries
Cheats' cheesecake 143–4
Raspberry clafoutis 142–3
Red lentil soup 122–3
red peppers
Basic tomato sauce 38–9
Cod with sweet peppers 83
Red pepper and polenta soldiers 40–1
Roasted butternut squash and red
pepper purée 29–30
reheating food 15, 17, 21–2
rice
Apricot rice pudding 98–9
Chickpea and rice batons 115–16
Chocolate rice pudding 97–8
Egg fried rice 134–5
leftover 135
Mango and coconut rice 96–7
Paella 176–7
Peachy pudding 55–6
Pork and apple with rice 50
Rice with butternut squash and
chickpeas 128–9
ricotta
Cheats' cheesecake 143–4
Spinach and ricotta lasagne 170
Roast carrot and parsnip fingers 35–6
Roast cauliflower 37–8
Roasted butternut squash and red pepper
purée 29–30
Roasted butternut squash with ginger 36–7
Rock cakes 190

Sage and onion sausages 135–6
salmon
Fish and tomato pie 84–6
Grilled fish with watercress sauce 84
Salmon and apple toast topper 164–5
Salmon and oat patties 132–3
Salmon and spring onion rösti 175–6
Salmon pâté 67–8
sandwiches 114, 164–5
sardines
Moroccan sardine balls in tomato
sauce 133–4
Sardine pâté 161
Scotch pancakes 111–12
Scrambled eggs 45–6
semolina
Baked Roman gnocchi 91–2
Simple fried fish 173–4
Simple vegetable or fruit purée 29–30
Soft polenta 141
soup
Cream of vegetable soup 72–3
Red lentil soup 122–3
Thick leek and potato soup 123–4
Soya bean and pea houmous 69–70
Spinach and ricotta lasagne 170
Spinach, pea and potato purée 33–4
spring onions
Salmon and spring onion rösti 175–6
Steamed or boiled vegetable sticks 35
strawberries
Cheats' cheesecake 143–4
Strawberry smoothie 194
sultanas
Apple and sultana overnight muesli
112–13
Pear and sultana purée 52–3
sweet potatoes
Haddock and sweet potato 46–7
Steamed or boiled vegetable sticks 35

Index

Sweet potato and avocado 31–2
Sweet potato and raisin muffins 147–8
Sweet potato gnocchi 139
Vegetarian cottage pie with sweet
  potato mash 77–8

Tagliatelle with green sauce 39–40
Thick leek and potato soup 123–4
tofu
  Japanese tofu patties 127–8
tomatoes
  Basic tomato sauce 38–9
  Cheese and tomato scone biscuits 100
  Fish and tomato pie 84–6
  Homemade ketchup 183–4
  Lamb shank with tomato and rosemary
    90–1
  Mackerel and tomato pasta 86–7
  Mild chilli 172
  Minced lamb hotpot 137–9
  Moroccan sardine balls in tomato sauce
    133–4
  Pasta with creamy tomato and butter
    bean sauce 130–1
  Quickest ever pizza 169–70
  Tomato and mushroom tortilla 82–3
  Vegetable and lentil bolognese
    171
traditional weaning 3, 4, 5, 25
Tropical fruit salad 99
trout
  Grilled fish with watercress
    sauce 84
Trout pasta salad 165–6
tuna
  Tuna carbonara 131–2
  Tuna meatballs 174–5
  Tuna melt wraps 162–3
Turkey and apple burgers 181–2

Vegetable and lentil bolognese 171
Vegetarian cottage pie with sweet potato
    mash 77–8
vitamin drops 12–13

walnuts
  Date and Walnut loaf 191–2
watercress
  Grilled fish with watercress
    sauce 84
  Mushroom and watercress pâté 161–2
Weetabix
  Homemade muesli 158–9
Wraps 70–1
  Tuna melt wraps 162–3

Yellow split pea dhal 44–5
yogurt
  Apple and squash dessert 54
  Avocado and yogurt dip 43
  Banana lassi 194
  Blueberry breakfast cake 159–60
  Salmon pâté 67–8
  Sweet potato and raisin muffins 147–8
  Yogurt dressing 76
Yorkshire pudding 94–5